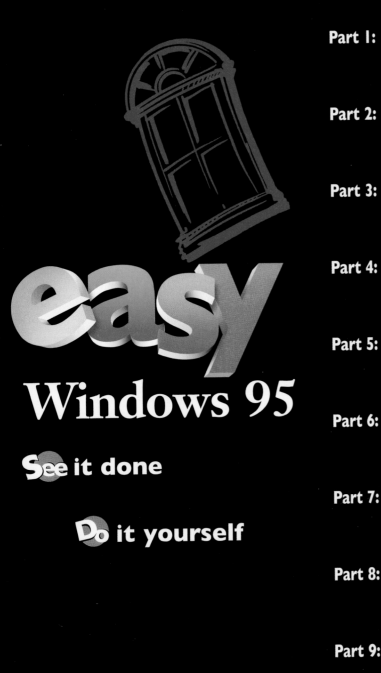

easy
Windows 95

See it done

Do it yourself

International Standard Book Number: 0-7897-1738-7

Library of Congress Catalog Card Number: 98-85581

01   00   99   98   4   3   2

Interpretation of the printing code: the rightmost double-digit number is the year of the book's printing; the rightmost single-digit, the number of the book's printing. For example, a printing code of 98-1 shows that the first printing of the book occurred in 1998.

Composed in Baker Signet by Macmillan Computer Publishing

Printed in the United States of America

President:	Richard K. Swadley
Publisher:	Dean Miller
Executive Editor:	Christopher Will
Director of Editorial Services	Carla Hall
Managing Editor:	Sarah Kearns
Indexing Manager:	Ginny Bess

About the Author

Shelley O'Hara works as a freelance writer in Indianapolis. She is the author of over 70 books and training manuals, including several best-selling titles. O'Hara is also the author of *Easy Windows 98*. She graduated with a BA in English from the University of South Carolina and also has an MA in English from the University of Maryland.

Dedication

To my aunt, Sunnya K. Dulin

Acknowledgments

Special thanks to Kate Shoup Welsh for another exceptional editing job. Thanks also to Chris Will for inviting me to do this project and to Brian Proffitt for this technical review.

Acquisitions Editor
Christopher Will

Development Editor
Kate Shoup Welsh

Project Editor
Kate Shoup Welsh

Copy Editor
Kate Shoup Welsh

Indexer
Chris Barrick

Technical Reviewer
Brian Proffitt

Editorial Coordinator
Mandie Rowell

Editorial Assistants
Jen Chisholm, Tracy Williams

Cover Designer
Anne Jones

Book Designer
Gary Adair, Jean Bisesi

Copy Writer
Eric Borgert

Production Supervisor
Tricia Flodder

Production Designer
Trina Wurst

Proofreader
Chris Livengood

How to Use This Book

It's as Easy as 1-2-3

Each part of this book is made up of a series of short, instructional lessons, designed to help you understand basic information that you need to get the most out of your computer hardware and software.

Click: Click the left mouse button once.

Double-click: Click the left mouse button twice in rapid succession.

Right-click: Click the right mouse button once.

Pointer Arrow: Highlights an item on the screen you need to point to or focus on in the step or task.

Selection: Highlights the area onscreen discussed in the step or task.

Click & Type: Click once where indicated and begin typing to enter your text or data.

Tips and Warnings give you a heads-up for any extra information you may need while working through the task.

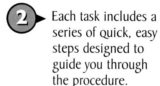

Each task includes a series of quick, easy steps designed to guide you through the procedure.

How to Drag: Point to the starting place or object. Hold down the mouse button (right or left per instructions), move the mouse to the new location, then release the button.

Each step is fully illustrated to show you how it looks onscreen.

Items that you select or click in menus, dialog boxes, tabs, and windows are shown in **Bold**. Information you type is in a `special font`.

Next Step: If you see this symbol, it means the task you're working on continues on the next page.

End Task: Task is complete.

Tasks

Task 1: Understanding the Desktop

Your computer desktop is a lot like your physical desktop; it contains tools to help you use your PC. Because the desktop is always your starting place, you should familiarize yourself with what appears on the desktop.

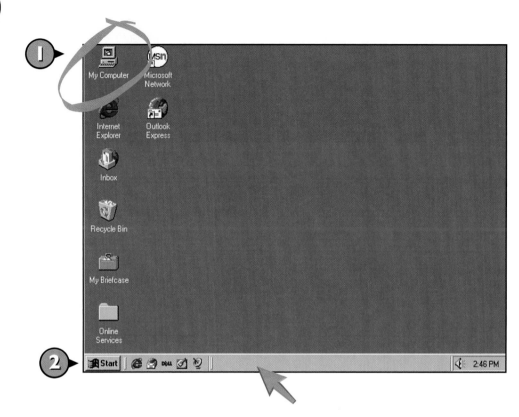

✓ You might see icons on your desktop that differ from the ones shown here. You can customize your desktop, adding icons for other programs, folders, printers, and so on. For information on customizing Windows, see Part 5, "Personalizing Windows."

 Point to the **My Computer** icon. This is the icon you use to display the contents of your system.

 Point to the *taskbar*. This bar displays the **Start** button (covered next) and buttons for each program that is running (in this case, none).

Task 2: Displaying the Start Menu

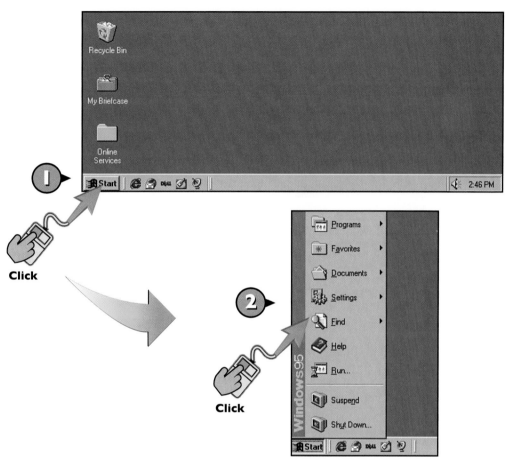

Click

Click

The *taskbar*, located at the bottom of your screen, contains the **Start** button. Clicking the **Start** button enables you to start applications, reopen documents you recently viewed, customize settings in Windows, get help, and more. You use the **Start** button to begin most tasks in Windows.

① ▶ Click the **Start** button.

② ▶ Click the command you want.

✓ If you click the **Start** button by mistake and want to close the **Start** menu without choosing a command, simply click outside the menu.

Task 3: Opening a Window

Windows 95 displays all its information in onscreen boxes called *windows*. To work with your computer, you must know how to display (or open) these windows. Most windows are represented onscreen by small pictures called *icons*. You can double-click an icon to display the contents of the window the icon represents.

✓ If nothing happens when you double-click an icon, it might be because you did not click quickly enough or because you single-clicked, moved the mouse, and single-clicked again. You have to click twice in rapid succession.

✓ If you have Internet Explorer 4 and your desktop is set up as a Web desktop (covered in Task 4, "Changing How the Contents of Windows are Displayed" in Part 3, "Working with Disks, Folders, and Files"), you can simply single-click to open an icon.

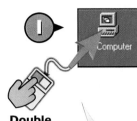

Double Click

 Double-click the **My Computer** icon.

 The contents of this icon are displayed, and a button for the **My Computer** window appears on the taskbar.

End Task

Task 4: Closing Windows

Start
Here

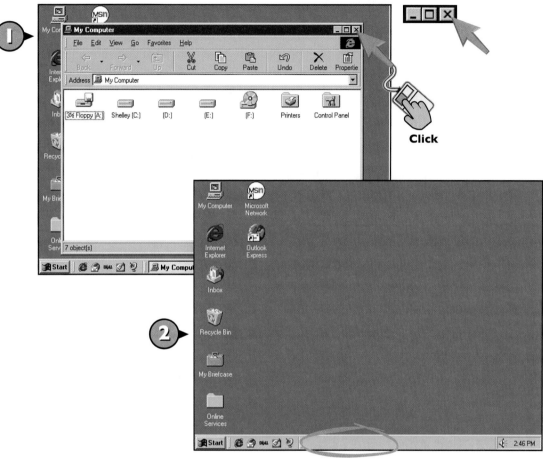

Click

You close a window after you finish working with it and its contents. Too many open windows clutter the desktop as well as the taskbar.

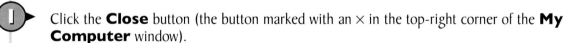

1. Click the **Close** button (the button marked with an × in the top-right corner of the **My Computer** window).

2. The window is closed, and the button for the window no longer appears in the taskbar.

✓ The **Control** menu, located in the upper-left corner of the title bar, contains commands related to the open window, such as **Restore, Move, Size, Close**, and so on. To close the window via the **Control** menu, click the **Control** menu icon and then choose **Close** from the menu. Alternatively, you can press **Alt+F4**.

Task 5: Minimizing a Window

You can reduce (minimize) a window so that it is still available as a toolbar button, but is not displayed on the desktop. You might want to minimize a window to temporarily move it out of your way but keep it active for later use.

Start Here

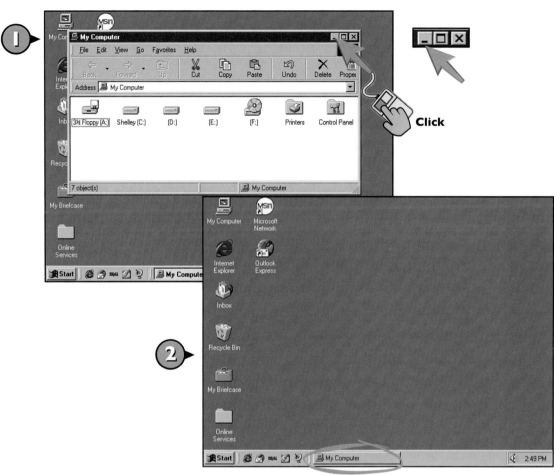

Click

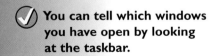
You can tell which windows you have open by looking at the taskbar.

1 ▶ Click the **Minimize** button in the window you want to minimize.

2 ▶ The window disappears from the desktop, but a button for the window remains on the taskbar.

End Task

Task 6: Maximizing a Window

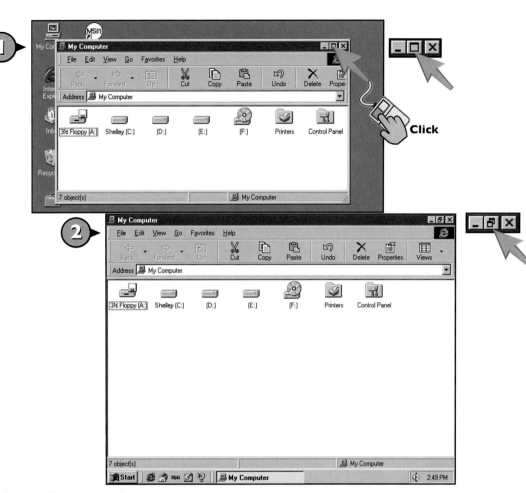

Click

You can enlarge (maximize) a window so that it fills the entire screen. Doing so gives you as much room as possible to work in that window.

 Click the **Maximize** button.

 The window enlarges to fill the screen, and the **Maximize** button changes to the **Restore** button.

 Keep in mind that when a window is maximized, it is as big as the screen and does not have any borders. You cannot resize or move a maximized window.

Task 7: Restoring a Window

If you maximize a window, you can easily restore it to its original size. You might want to restore a window so that you can manually resize it.

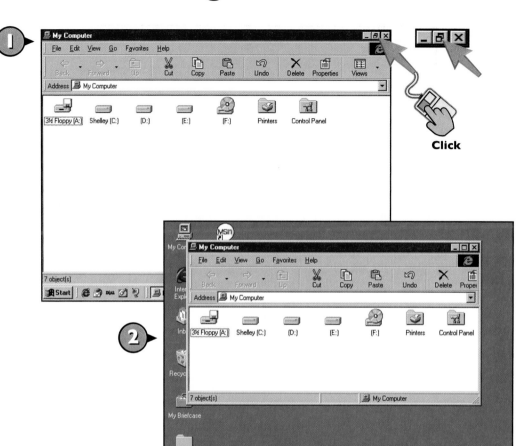

Click

1 In a maximized window, click the **Restore** button.

2 The window is restored to its original size.

Task 8: Moving a Window

Start Here

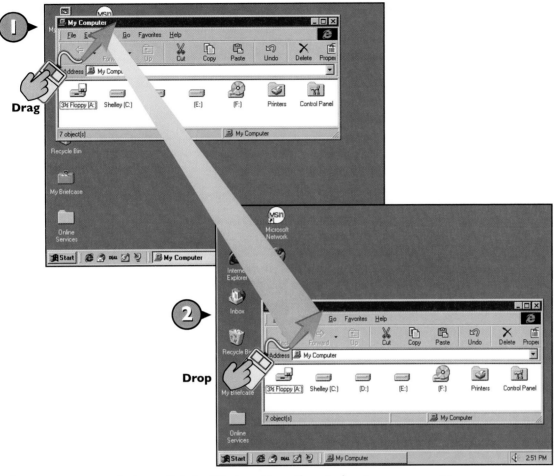

Drag

Drop

As you add more applications, folders, shortcuts, and so on to the desktop, you'll need more room to display these elements. You can easily move the windows around so you can see all the open windows at one time.

1 ▶ To move an open window, click its title bar. Drag the window to a new position.

2 ▶ Release the mouse button. The window and its contents appear in the new location.

 Be sure to point to the title bar. If you point to any other area, you might resize the window instead of moving it.

Task 9: Resizing a Window

In addition to being able to move a window, you can resize a window to whatever size you want. Resizing windows is helpful if you want to view more than one window at the same time.

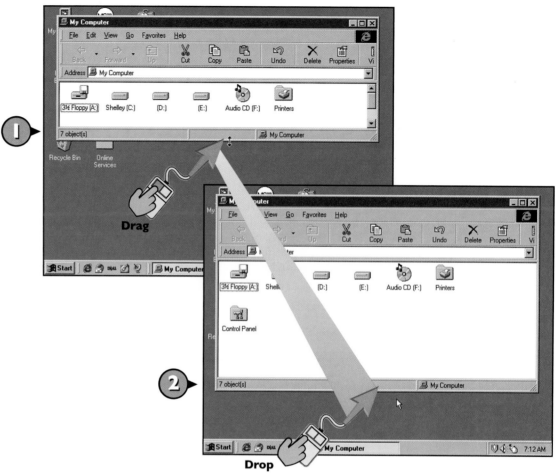

✓ You can drag a corner of the window to proportionally resize both dimensions (height and width) at the same time.

✓ You cannot resize a window that is maximized. If you don't see borders, you cannot resize the window. If you want to resize a maximized window, simply restore it and then resize it.

1 ▶ Point to any window border. You should see a double-headed arrow. Drag the border to resize the window.

2 ▶ Release the mouse button. The window is resized.

Task 10: Scrolling a Window

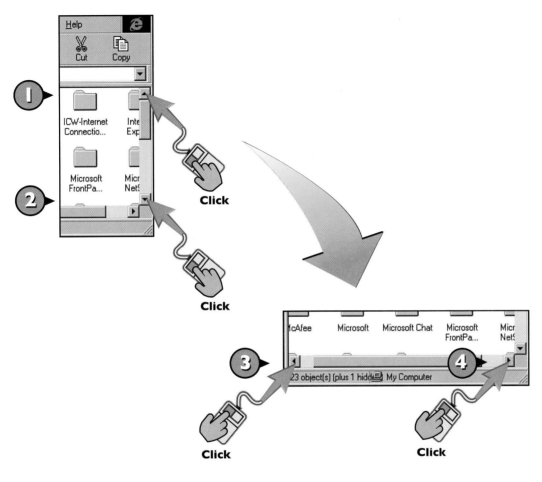

If a window is too small to show all its contents, horizontal and vertical *scrollbars* appear along the edges of the window. You can use these bars to scroll through the window to see the other contents.

Click

Click

Click

Click

Click the up arrow to scroll up through the window.

Click the down arrow to scroll down through the window.

Click the left arrow to scroll left through the window.

Click the right arrow to scroll right through the window.

You can click anywhere in the scrollbar to jump in that direction to another part of the window. You can also drag the scroll box to scroll quickly through the window.

Task 11: Using Menus

Although you can perform many tasks by clicking various onscreen objects, you must choose *commands* to perform the majority of Windows tasks. Commands are organized in *menus* to make them easy to find. Most windows contain menu bars that list the available menus; each menu then contains a group of related commands.

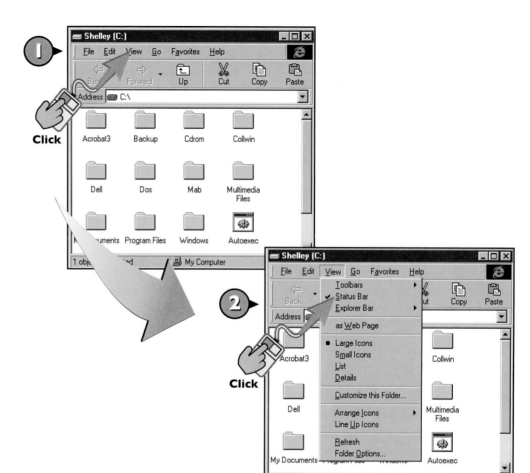

✓ Selecting a command that is accompanied by an arrow will display a *submenu*. Clicking a command that is followed by an ellipsis will display a *dialog box*.

✓ To close a menu without making a selection, press the **Esc** button on your keyboard or click outside the menu.

1 ▶ In the window or program, click the menu name (in this case, the menu name is **View**).

2 ▶ Click the command you want.

Task 12: Using Shortcut Menus

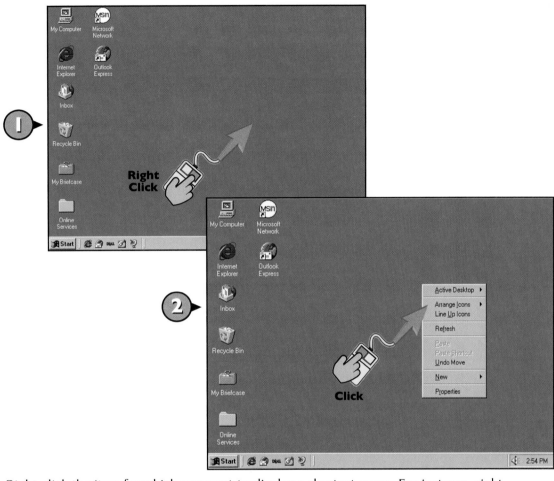

Shortcut menus, also called *quick menus* and *pop-up menus,* provide common commands related to the selected item. You can, for example, quickly copy and paste, create a new folder, move a file, or rearrange icons using a shortcut menu.

① ▶ Right-click the item for which you want to display a shortcut menu. For instance, right-click any blank part of the desktop.

② ▶ Click the command you want.

✅ **Different shortcut menus appear depending on what you're pointing to when you right-click the mouse.**

When you choose certain commands, a *dialog box* appears to prompt you for additional information about how to carry out the command. Dialog boxes are used throughout Windows; luckily, all dialog boxes have common elements and all are treated in a similar way.

✓ Dialog boxes contain various types of elements, including *radio buttons* and *check boxes*. You can choose only one radio button within a group of radio buttons; choosing a second option deselects the first. However, you can select multiple check boxes within a group of check boxes.

✓ When a dialog box is open, you cannot perform any other action until you accept changes by clicking the **OK** button. To effect changes without closing the dialog box, click the **Apply** button. To close the dialog box without making a selection, click the **Cancel** button.

Task 13: Using a Dialog Box

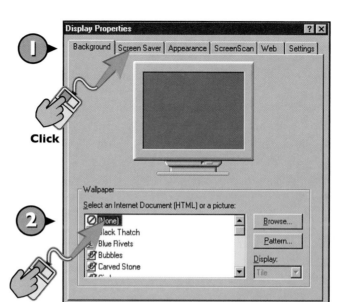

Click

Click

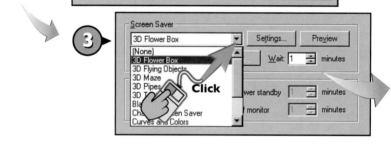

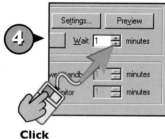

Click

Click

① To view a *tab*, click it.

② To use a *list box*, scroll through the list, and click the item you want.

③ To use a *drop-down list box*, click the down-arrow button to the right of the *text box* and then click the desired item.

④ To use a *spin box*, click the arrows to increment or decrement the value, or type a value in the text box.

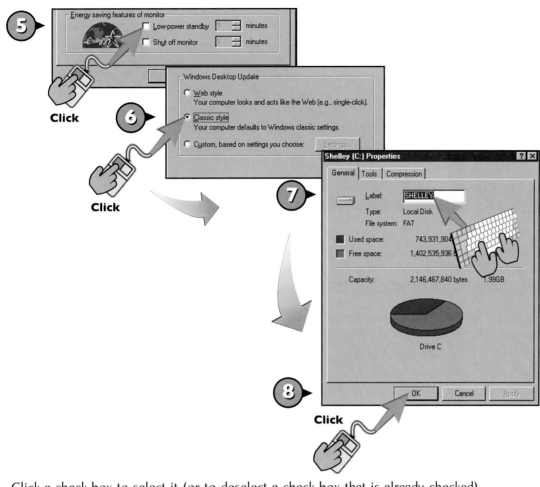

Click

Click

Click

Click

5 ▸ Click a check box to select it (or to deselect a check box that is already checked).

6 ▸ Click a radio button to activate it (or to deactivate a radio button that is already activated).

7 ▸ Type an entry in a text box.

8 ▸ After you make your selections, click the **OK** button.

Task 14: Arranging Windows on the Desktop

As you work, you will often have several windows open on the desktop at one time. The windows probably overlap each other, which can make it difficult to find what you want. To make your work easier and more efficient, Windows enables you to arrange the windows on the desktop in several different ways.

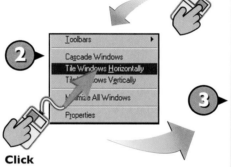

Right Click

Click

 To work in any one of the open windows, click the desired window to activate it. The active window moves to the front of the stack, and its title bar is a different color.

 Be sure to right-click a blank area of the taskbar, not a taskbar button.

1 With multiple windows on the desktop, right-click a blank area of the taskbar.

2 Click the arrangement you want from the shortcut menu.

3 Windows arranges the windows; here they are tiled horizontally.

 Next Step

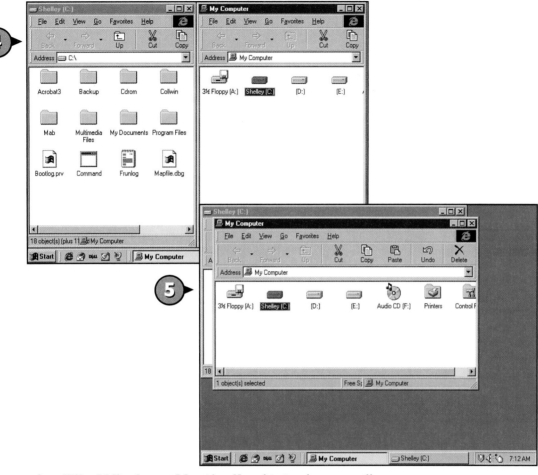

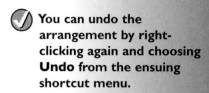

4 ▶ If you select **Tile Windows Vertically**, this is what you will see.

5 ▶ If you select **Cascade Windows**, this is what you will see.

✓ **You can undo the arrangement by right-clicking again and choosing Undo from the ensuing shortcut menu.**

End Task

Use the **Contents** tab in the **Help** window to locate help for performing specific procedures, such as printing a document or installing new software. The specific topics included in the **Contents** tab quickly refer you to everyday tasks you might need to perform in the program.

Task 15: Looking Up a Help Topic in the Table of Contents

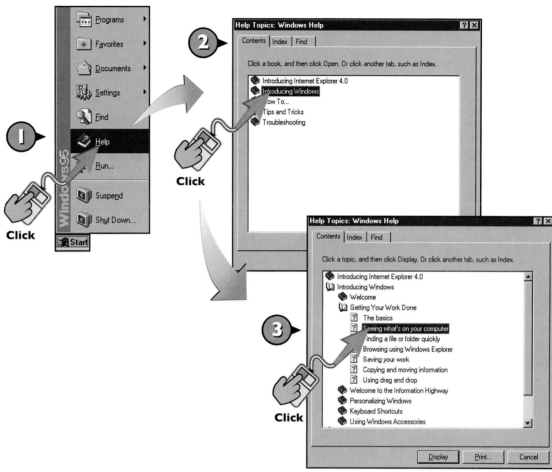

✓ **Click the Options button and then choose Print to print the help topic.**

✓ **You can click any of the underlined text in the help area to display a definition of that term or to display related help information.**

1 ▸ Click the **Start** button, then select **Help**.

2 ▸ The **Contents** tab of the **Windows Help** window is visible by default. Click the topic you want help on.

3 ▸ Continue clicking book topics until you find the exact help topic you need, and then click that help topic.

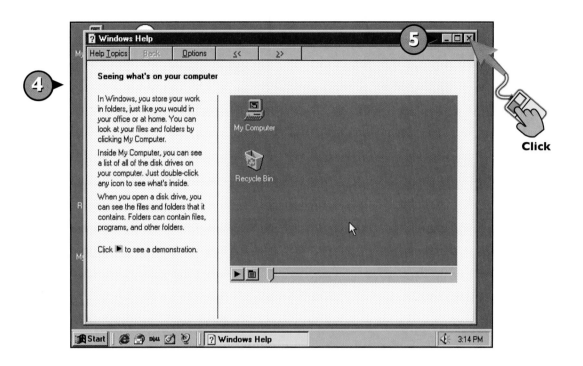

Click

(4) Review the help information.

(5) Click the **Close** button to close the **Help** window.

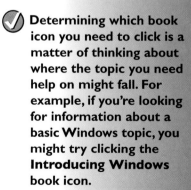

Determining which book icon you need to click is a matter of thinking about where the topic you need help on might fall. For example, if you're looking for information about a basic Windows topic, you might try clicking the **Introducing Windows** book icon.

End Task

Task 16: Looking Up a Help Topic in the Index

If you want to find help on a specific topic, such as storing files by size or editing text, use the **Index** tab in the **Help** window. Topics listed in the index are in alphabetical order. You can quickly scroll to see topics of interest.

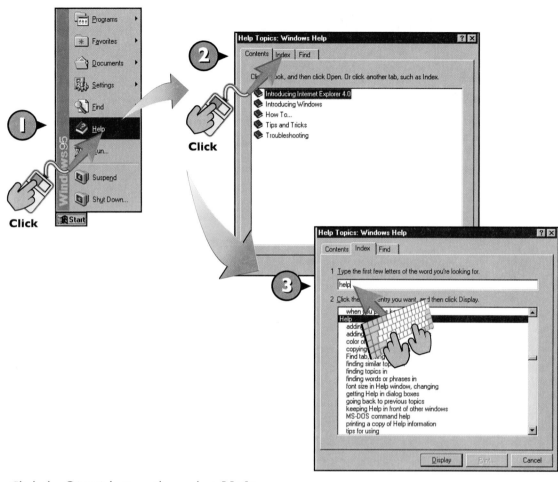

Click

Click

✓ You can scroll through the list of topics on the **Index** tab. You can also click the **Back** button to go back to the previous help page.

1 ▶ Click the **Start** button, then select **Help**.

2 ▶ The **Contents** tab of the **Windows Help** window is visible by default. Click the **Index** tab.

3 ▶ Type the topic for which you want to find help. The list below the text field jumps to the topic you type.

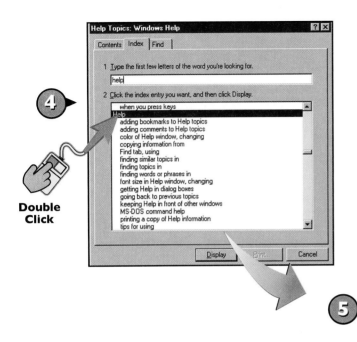

Double Click

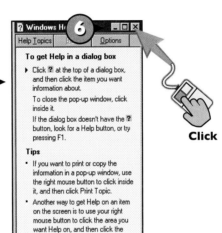

Click

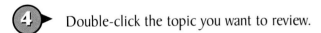

Double-click the topic you want to review.

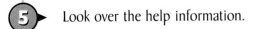

Look over the help information.

Click the **Close** button.

Task 17: Searching for a Help Topic

If you don't find the topic in the table of contents or index, try searching for it within Windows Help using the Find tool. Windows will display a list of topics that contain what you are looking for; you can then select the one you want.

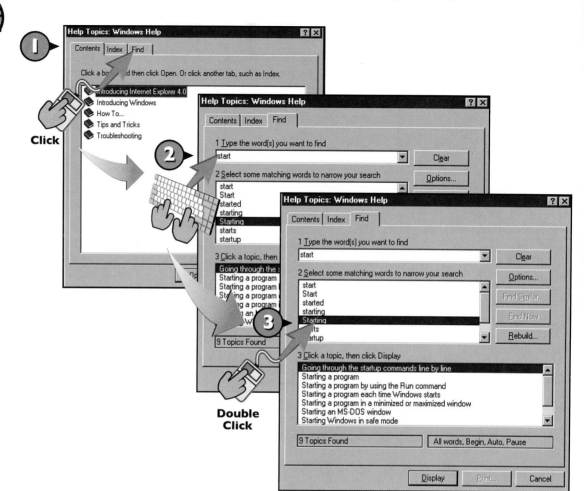

Click

Double Click

✓ Windows Help works in the same way throughout most Windows applications. If you master help basics, you can apply these same skills to other programs.

✓ The first time you use the Find tab, you will be prompted to set up the word list. Follow the steps in the Find Setup wizard.

1 ▶ Click the **Find** tab in the **Windows Help** dialog box. (To get to this dialog box, refer to Task 15.)

2 ▶ Type the topic you want to find.

3 ▶ In the middle of the dialog box, narrow your search by selecting the best match from the list of matches.

Next Step

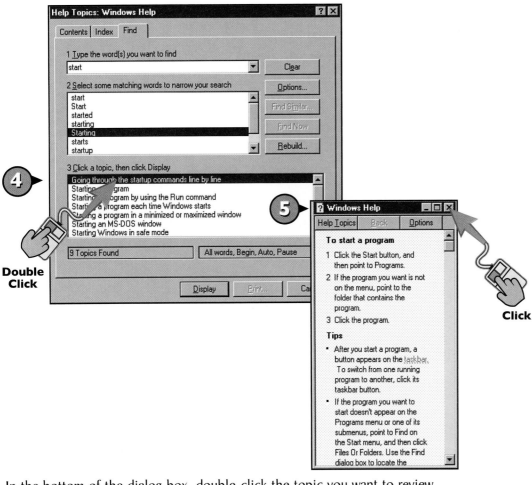

Double Click

Click

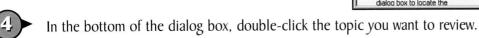

4 In the bottom of the dialog box, double-click the topic you want to review.

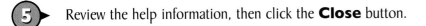

5 Review the help information, then click the **Close** button.

End Task

Task 18: Getting Context-Sensitive Help

When you open a dialog box, you might not know what each of the options do. If you have a question about an option, you can view a description of that option by following the steps in this task.

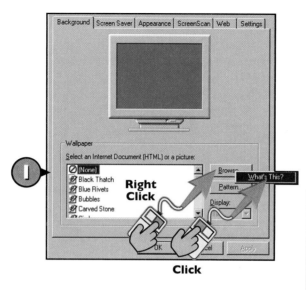

Start Here

Right Click

Click

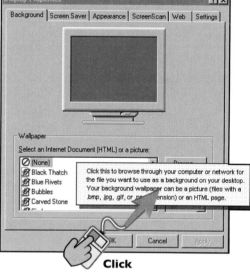

Click this to browse through your computer or network for the file you want to use as a background on your desktop. Your background wallpaper can be a picture (files with a .bmp, .jpg, .gif, or other extension) or an HTML page.

Click

 In a dialog box, right-click the option you want help on, and then click the **What's This?** button.

 After you review the material in the pop-up explanation, click anywhere within the dialog box to close the pop-up box.

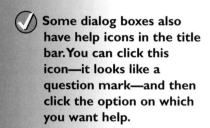

Some dialog boxes also have help icons in the title bar. You can click this icon—it looks like a question mark—and then click the option on which you want help.

End Task

Task 19: Shutting Down the Computer

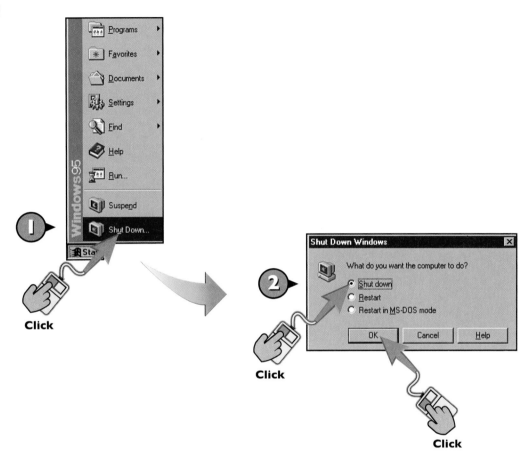

Click

Click

Click

If you turn off the power to your computer before you properly shut the computer down, you could lose valuable data or damage an open file. Windows provides a safe shutdown feature that checks for open programs and files, warns you to save unsaved files, and prepares the program for you to turn off your computer. You should always shut down before you turn off the power.

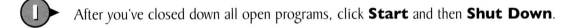

① After you've closed down all open programs, click **Start** and then **Shut Down**.

② After you select the **Shut down** radio button, click **OK**.

✓ Sometimes you might need to work from **DOS** instead of Windows. To boot to DOS, choose the **Restart in MS-DOS** mode option in the **Shut Down Windows** dialog box, and then choose **Yes**. You can also choose **Restart** to restart the computer.

✓ The **Suspend** command is most pertinent to portable computers. You can suspend the PC to conserve energy.

Using Applications in Windows 95

One advantage of using Windows is the enormous number of available Windows applications. You can use many word-processing, database, spreadsheet, drawing, and other programs in Windows. This variety of applications provides you with all the tools you need to perform your everyday tasks.

Windows applications are easy to open and use, and enable you to save data in files of different names and in various locations on your hard disk or on a floppy disk. You can open a file at any time to view, edit, or print it. This part covers starting and working with applications.

Tasks

Task 1: Starting an Application from the Start Menu

Most of the time you spend using your computer will be with an application. You can start an application in any number of ways, including from the **Start** menu. When you install a new Windows application, that program's installation procedure will usually set up a program folder and program icon on the **Start** menu.

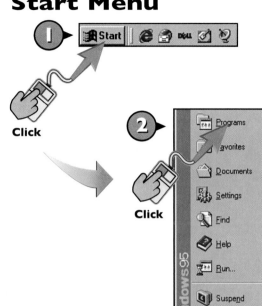

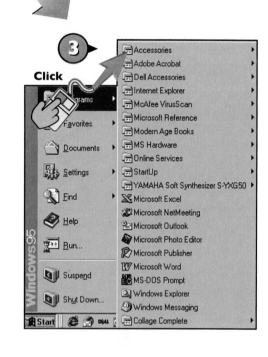

✅ To close the **Start** menu without making a choice, simply click outside the menu.

✅ If you don't see your program icon listed, you can easily add programs to the **Start** menu. For more information about how to handle this, see Part 6, "Setting Up Programs."

1 ▶ Click the **Start** button.

2 ▶ Click the **Programs** command.

3 ▶ Click the folder that contains the application you want to start (in this case, the **Accessories** folder).

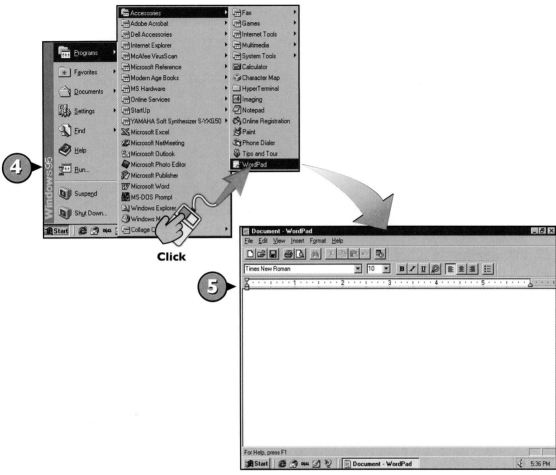

Click

④ ▶ Click the application you want to start (in this case, WordPad).

⑤ ▶ The application opens in its own window.

Task 2: Starting an Application from a Shortcut Icon

If you frequently use a certain program, you might want to be able to access that program right from the desktop. To do so, you can set up a shortcut icon (covered in Part 6) and then start the program by double-clicking that icon.

Double Click

 If nothing happens when you double-click the icon, or if the icon moves, it might be because you haven't clicked quickly enough or because you clicked and dragged by accident. Be sure to press the mouse button twice quickly.

 Double-click the shortcut icon on the desktop.

2 The application (in this case, Microsoft Word) is started and displayed in its own window.

End Task

Task 3: Switching Between Applications

Because you most likely work with more than one type of document, you need a way to switch from one program to another. For example, you might want to compare price figures from an Excel worksheet with a price list you've set up in Word. Switching between applications enables you not only to compare data, but also to share data.

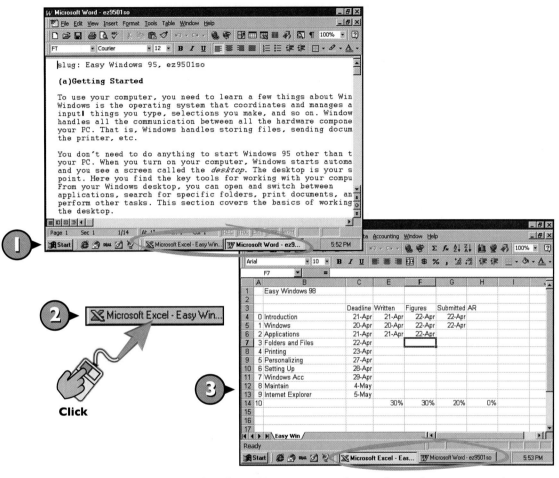

Click

✓ The number of programs you can have open at any one time depends on the amount of **RAM** (random-access memory) in your system.

1. After you start two programs, note that the taskbar contains a button for each program. In this case, the **Microsoft Word** button is selected, and Microsoft Word is displayed onscreen.

2. Click the button for the program you want to switch to (in this case, Microsoft Excel).

3. Excel becomes the active program.

✓ You can tell what programs are open by looking at the taskbar. Each open program is represented by a button; the button representing the program you are currently using is selected.

Task 4: Closing an Application

When you finish working in an application, close it to free system memory. Too many open applications can tax your system's memory and slow the computer's processes, such as saving, printing, switching between applications, and so on.

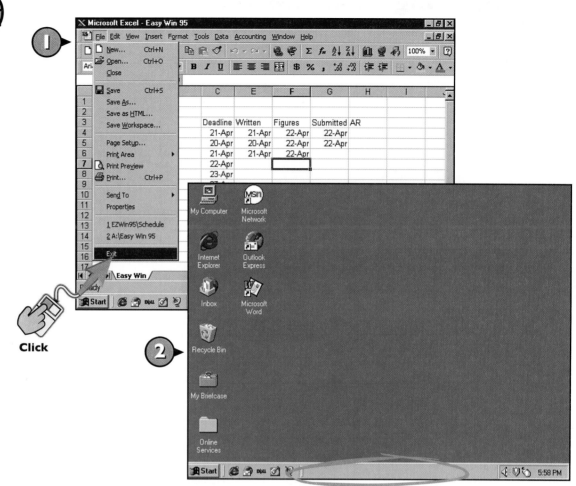

 To close an application, you can also press **Alt+F4** or click the **Close** button in the application's title bar.

 If you have not saved a file and choose to close that file's application, a message box appears asking if you want to save the file. If you do, click **Yes**; if not, click **No**. If you want to return to the document, click **Cancel**. For more information, see Task 8, "Saving a Document," later in this part.

Click

① Click **File** and then click **Exit**.

② The program is closed. Notice that the **Excel** taskbar button has disappeared.

End Task

Task 5: Starting an Application and Opening a Document

Start Here

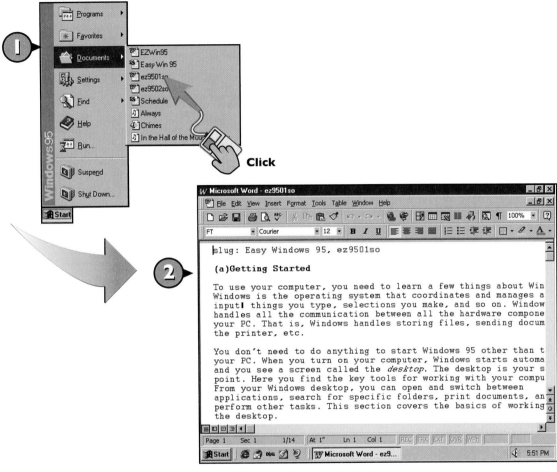

Click

If you want to work on a document that you recently had open (in Word, for example), you can use a shortcut to both start Word and open the document. Windows 95's **Documents** menu lists the 15 documents that you have opened most recently.

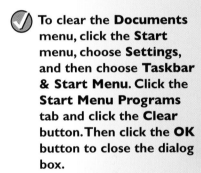
To clear the **Documents** menu, click the **Start** menu, choose **Settings**, and then choose **Taskbar & Start Menu**. Click the **Start Menu Programs** tab and click the **Clear** button. Then click the **OK** button to close the dialog box.

Click the **Start** button, click Documents, and then click the document you want to work on (in this case, **ez9501so**).

The program for that document is started, and the document is opened.

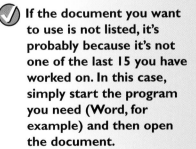
If the document you want to use is not listed, it's probably because it's not one of the last 15 you have worked on. In this case, simply start the program you need (Word, for example) and then open the document.

End Task

Task 6: Closing a Document

When you save a document, it remains open so that you can continue working. You can close the document when you are done working on it. Closing documents you no longer use frees up memory.

Click

✓ If you click the **Close** button on the program window, you exit the program. Also, remember that the document window has its own set of window controls—separate from the controls for the program window. You can move, resize, maximize, minimize, and close the document window using the skills you learned in Part I.

1 ▶ Click the **Close** button in the document window.

2 ▶ The document is closed, but the program remains open. You can create a new document or open an existing document.

Task 7: Creating a New Document

Start Here

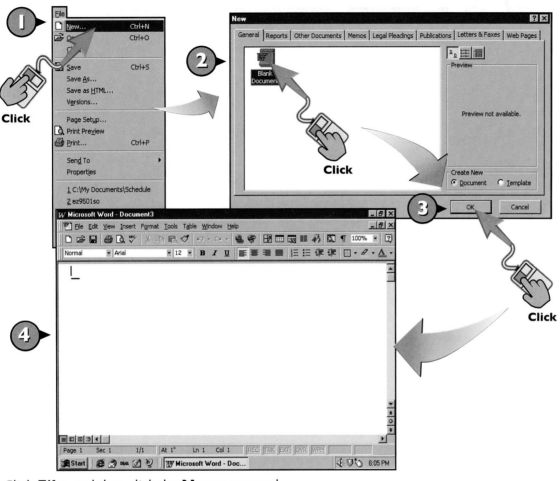

Click

Click

Click

When you want to start your work with a new "sheet" of paper, you can create a new document. For complex programs like PowerPoint (a presentation program) and Access (a database program), you might be prompted to make some selections before the new document is created. For others, you simply select the template you want. (A *template* is a predesigned document.)

1. Click **File**, and then click the **New** command.

2. If you see a **New** dialog box, click the type of document you want to create.

3. Click the **OK** button.

4. A new document is displayed.

✓ As a shortcut in many programs, you can click the **New** button to create a new document based on the default template.

End Task

Task 8: Saving a Document

You save documents and files so that you can refer to them later. The first time you save a file, you must assign that file a name and a folder (that is, a location).

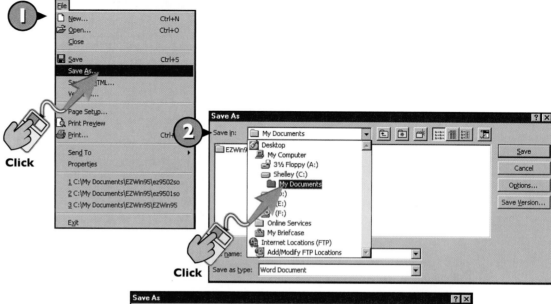

After you've saved and named a file, you can simply click **File** and select **Save** to resave that file to the same location with the same name. Any changes you have made since the last save are reflected in the file.

To save the file with a different name or in a different location, use the **Save As** command and enter a different filename or folder.

You can use spaces, letters, and numbers in filenames, but you cannot use any of the following characters:

: " ? * < > / \ |

1. ▶ Click **File**, and then click the **Save As** command.

2. ▶ Click the **Save in** drop-down list and select the drive and folder in which you want to save the file.

3. ▶ To save the document in a subfolder, click the desired folder in the list.

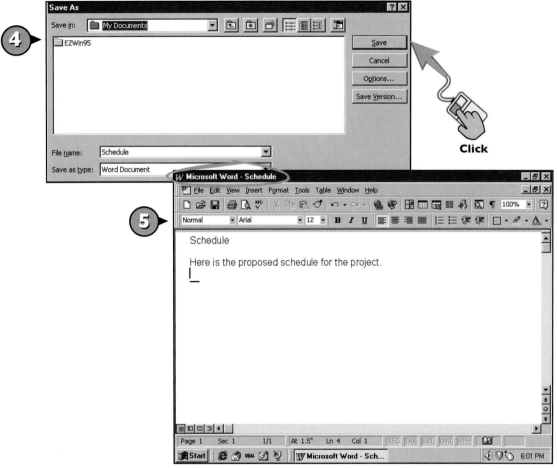

Click

④ Click the **Save** button.

⑤ The application saves the file and returns to the document window. The document name is listed in the title bar.

✓ The program might propose a name for the file. You can either accept this name or type a new name.

✓ To move up through the folder structure, click the **Up One Level** button, and then double-click the folder you want.

Task 9: Opening an Existing Document

The purpose of saving a document is to make it available for later use. You can open any of the documents you have saved by selecting **File** and choosing the **Open** command.

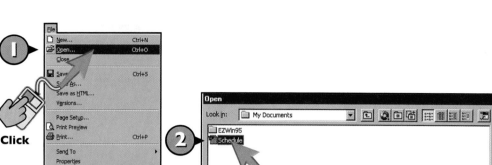

Click

Double Click

✓ If you can't find the file you want to work with, it could be because you did not save it where you thought you did. Try looking in a different drive or folder. If you still can't find it, try searching for the file (for more information about searching for files, see Part 3, "Working with Disks, Folders, and Files").

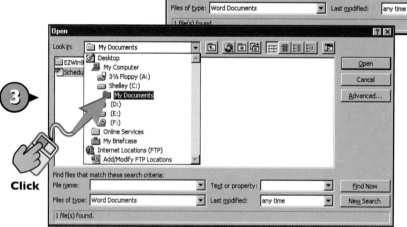

Click

1 Click **File** and then click the **Open** command.

2 If the file you need is listed in the dialog box, double-click it and skip the remaining steps.

3 If the file is stored on another drive, display the **Look in** drop-down list and select the drive where you placed the file.

Next Step

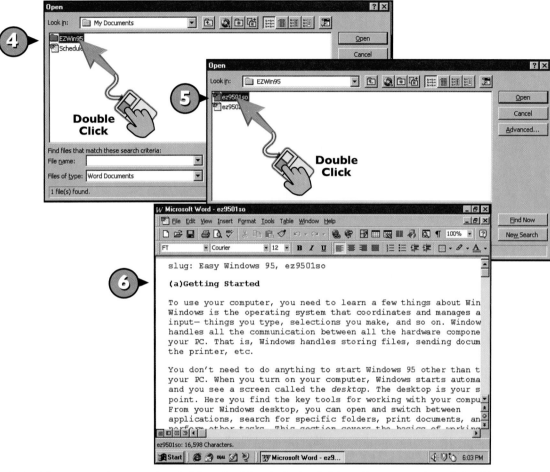

4 If the file is stored in another folder, double-click the folder where you placed the file. You can use the **Up One Level** button to move up through the folder structures.

5 When you find the file you seek, double-click it.

6 The file is opened.

✓ **As a shortcut, click File. You'll notice that the last files opened are listed near the bottom of the menu. You can open any of these files by clicking them in the File menu.**

Task 10: Switching Between Open Documents

Just as you can work with several sheets of paper on your desk, you can work with several documents in your application. You can open as many documents as the program allows. Simply click **File** and select the **Open** command to open the files you want to work with. Then you can easily switch between any of the open documents.

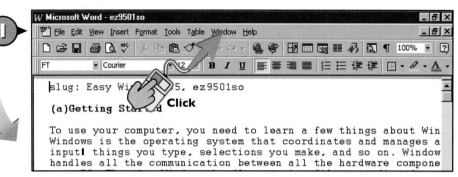

Click

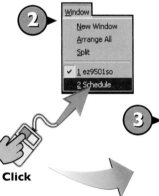

Click

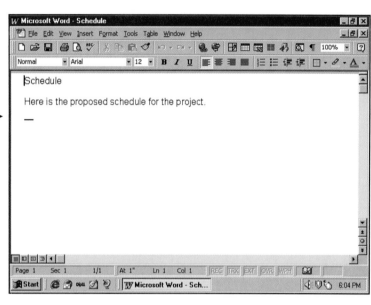

✓ Don't confuse switching between documents with switching between programs. To switch among programs, use the taskbar. For more information, refer to Task 3, "Switching Between Applications."

✓ Some programs (such as WordPad) don't allow you to have more than one document open. When you create a new document or open another document, the current document is closed.

1 ▶ Click **Window**.

2 ▶ Notice that the current document has a check mark next to its name. Click the document that you want to switch to (in this case, **Schedule**).

3 ▶ The document you just clicked in the **Window** menu becomes the active document.

Task 11: Selecting Text

Start Here

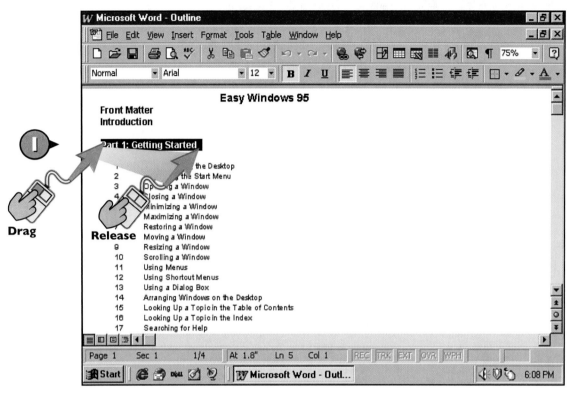

Drag

Release

One of the primary skills you need to develop for working with data is selecting what you want to work on. For instance, you can select text and then delete it, move it, copy it, change its appearance, and more.

Click at the start of the text you want to select. Hold down the left mouse button, drag across the text, then release the mouse button. The selected text appears highlighted.

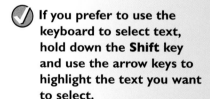
If you prefer to use the keyboard to select text, hold down the **Shift** key and use the arrow keys to highlight the text you want to select.

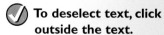
To deselect text, click outside the text.

End Task

Task 12: Copying Text

One of the most common editing tasks is to copy text. You can copy text and paste the copy in the current document or in another document.

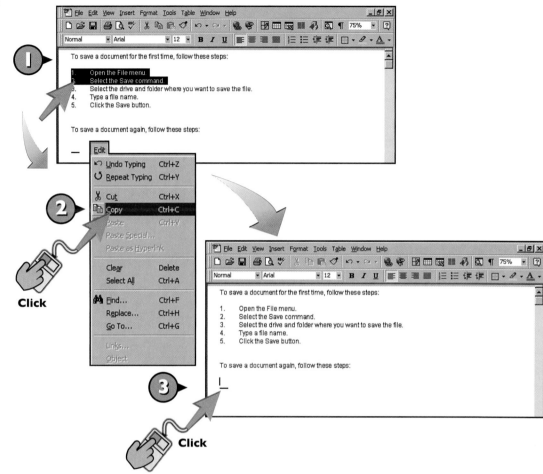

Start Here

Click

Click

(✓) To copy data from one open document to another, select the text and then move to the document where you want to paste the text using the **Window** menu.

(✓) Many programs have shortcuts for copying and pasting data. Look for **Copy** and **Paste** buttons on the toolbar. You can also use keyboard shortcuts (usually **Ctrl+C** for copy and **Ctrl+V** for paste).

1 ▶ Select the text you want to copy.

2 ▶ Click **Edit**, and then select the **Copy** command.

3 ▶ Click the spot in the document where you want to put the copied data.

Next Step ▶

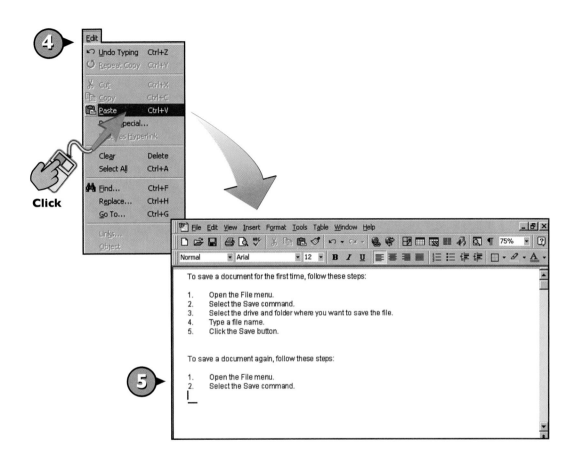

Click

For information about
copying data from one
application to another, see
Task 14, "Copying Data
Between Applications."

 Click **Edit**, and then select the **Paste** command.

 The data is pasted into the document.

You can undo a paste
operation if you change
your mind after
performing the action.
Simply click **Edit** and then
select the **Undo Paste**
command to remove the
text you just pasted.

Task 13: Moving Text

Just as you can copy text, you can move text from one location in a document to another location in the same document. You can also move text from one document to another. Moving text is similar to copying text, except that when you move something it is deleted from its original location.

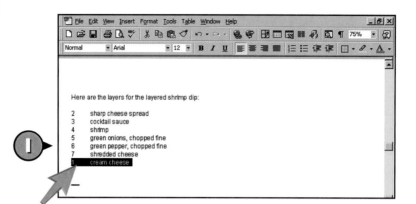

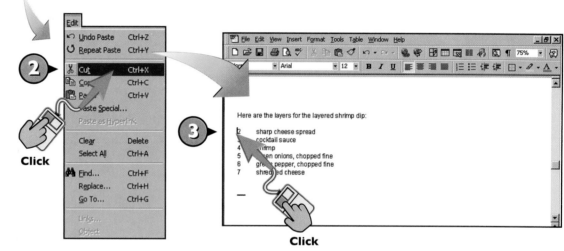

Click

Click

✓ For help on moving data from one application to another, see Task 15, "Moving Data Between Applications."

✓ Many programs have shortcuts for cutting and pasting data. Look for Cut and Paste buttons in the toolbar. You can also use keyboard shortcuts (usually **Ctrl+X** for Cut and **Ctrl+V** for Paste).

1 ▶ Select the text you want to move.

2 ▶ Click **Edit**, and then click the **Cut** command. Windows deletes the data from the document and places it in the **Clipboard**, a temporary holding spot.

3 ▶ Click in the document where you want to place the text.

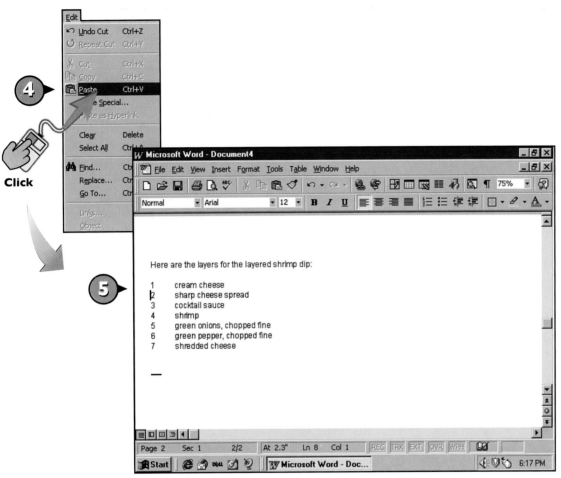

Click

④ Click **Edit**, and then select the **Paste** command.

⑤ The text is pasted into the new location.

Task 14: Copying Data Between Applications

You can copy data from a document in one application and paste it into another document in another application to save time typing. In addition to being able to copy text, you can copy spreadsheets, figures, charts, clip art, and so on. Using copied text and graphics saves you time in your work.

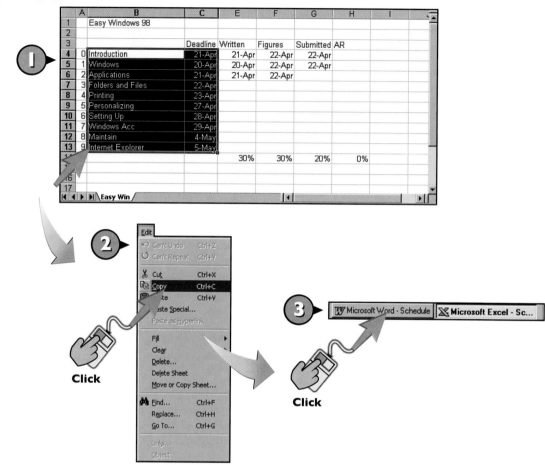

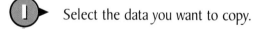

✓ For some programs, you can select how the data is pasted. For instance, if you copy an Excel worksheet to Word, you can paste the data as a table or as an Excel worksheet.

✓ If the **Paste** command is grayed out, it means you have not copied anything. Be sure to click **Edit** and then select the **Copy** command before you try to paste the text.

1 ▶ Select the data you want to copy.

2 ▶ Click **Edit**, and then click the **Copy** command.

3 ▶ Click the taskbar button representing the program you want to switch to (in this case, Microsoft Word). If the program isn't started, start the program.

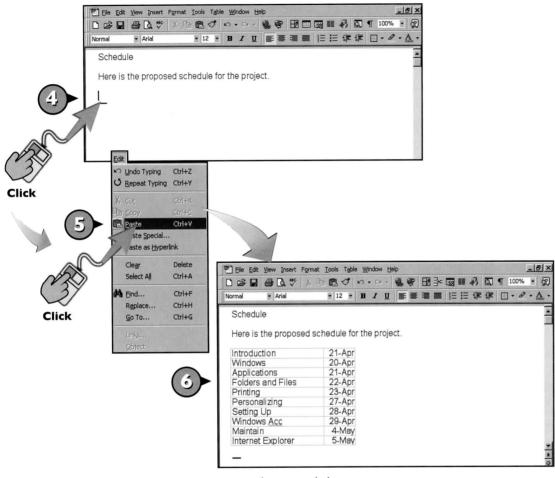

Click

Click

Click the location where you want to paste the copied data.

Click **Edit**, and then click the **Paste** command.

The data is pasted into the document.

Task 15: Moving Data Between Applications

Just as you can copy information from one application to another, you can also move information from one application to another. For instance, you can cut a table of numerical data from Excel and paste into a report in Word.

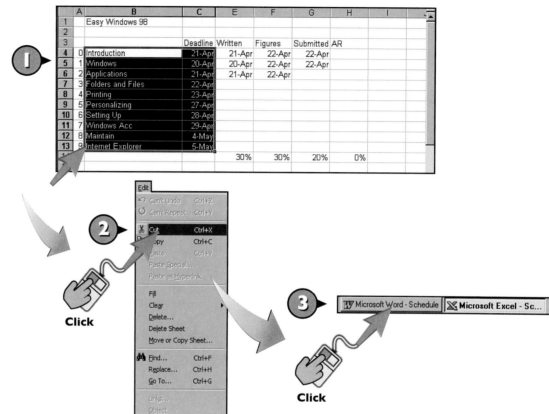

Click

Click

✅ The data is pasted into the document in an acceptable format. For instance, if you cut Excel data and paste it into a Word document, it is inserted as a table. You can also use a special command to paste it as a spreadsheet. See the next task.

 Select the data you want to move.

 Click **Edit**, and then click the **Cut** command. Windows deletes the data from the document and places it in the **Clipboard**, a temporary holding spot.

 Click the taskbar button representing the program you want to switch to (in this case, Microsoft Word).

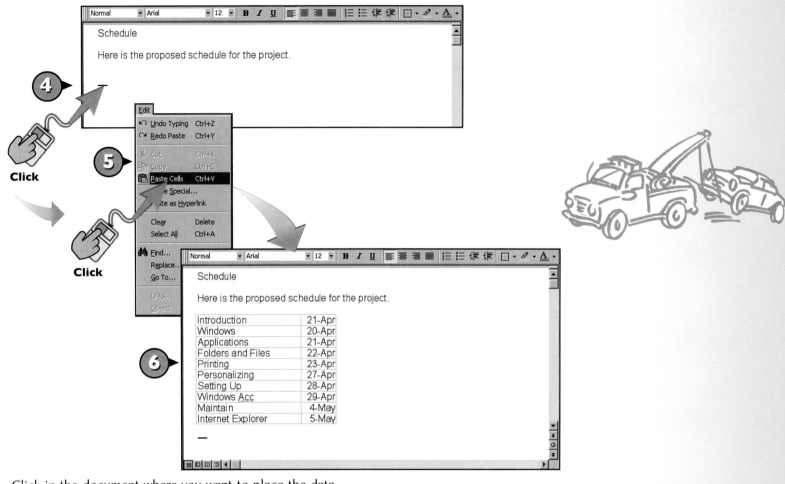

4 Click in the document where you want to place the data.

5 Click **Edit**, and then click the **Paste** command. (The name of this command may vary, depending on what you have selected to cut and paste.)

6 The data is pasted into the document.

Task 16: Linking Data Between Applications

You might link data between applications if you want the data to be updated automatically when you edit or add to the source document. Linking data saves you time because you only have to edit the information once; Windows then updates any linked files for you.

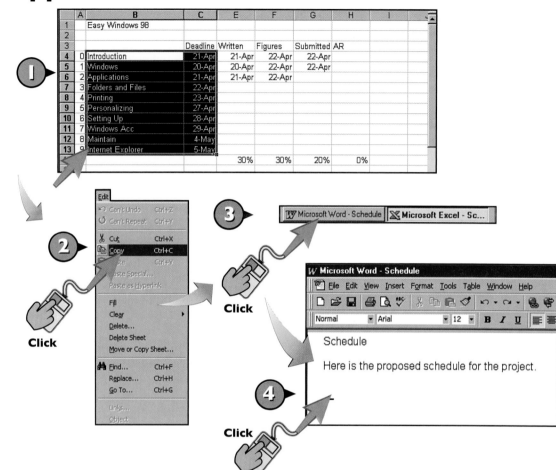

You can embed an object from another program type. To do so, click the **Object** command in the **Insert** menu. From the list of object types, choose the application in which you want to create the data. Create the document, and then click the **OK** button.

The available formats depend on the type of data you're pasting and control how the data is inserted into the document.

1. In the source document, select the data you want to link.

2. Click **Edit**, and then click the **Copy** command.

3. Click the taskbar button representing the program and document where you want to paste the linked data.

4. Click in the document where you want the linked data to go.

Next Step

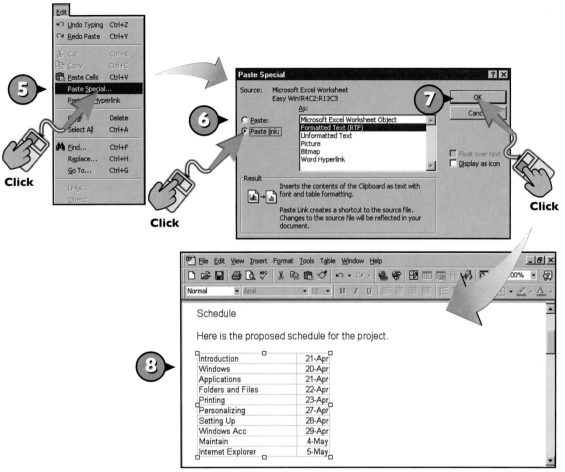

5 ▶ Click **Edit**, and then click the **Paste Special** command.

6 ▶ Select the **Paste Link** radio button, and then select the format you want to paste from the **As** list box.

7 ▶ Click the **OK** button.

8 ▶ Windows inserts the data with a link between the destination and the source files.

3

Working with Disks, Folders, and Files

One part of working with Windows is learning how to work with the documents you save and store on your system. Think of your computer's hard drive as a filing cabinet. To keep your files organized, you can set up *folders*. Folders on the hard drive represent drawers in the filing cabinet, and each folder can hold files or other folders. (In previous versions of Windows, folders were called *directories*.) You can open and close folders, view a folder's contents, copy and move folders, and create or delete folders.

The more you work on your computer, the more files and folders you add. After a while, your computer will become cluttered, and you'll need a way to keep these files organized. Windows provides features that can help you find, organize, and manage your files. You can copy, move, and delete files, and more. For working with files and folders, you can use either **My Computer** or **Windows Explorer**, as covered in this section.

Tasks

Task 1: Opening Folders

Folders contain files, programs, and other items that you can use to work in Windows. You can display the contents of a folder to work with the files—move a file, create a shortcut icon, start a program, and so on.

Start Here

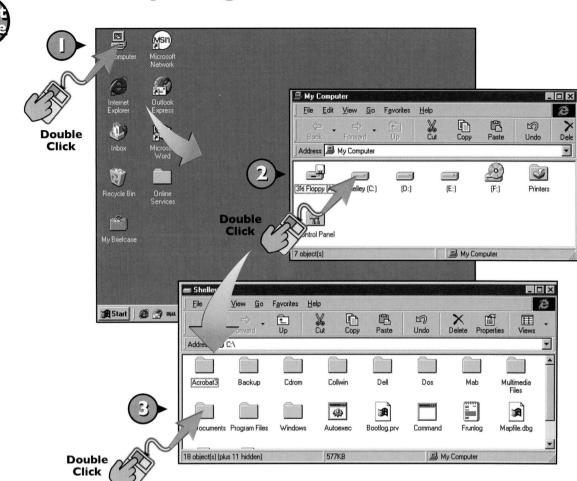

Double Click

Double Click

Double Click

✓ Remember that you can use the scrollbars to scroll through the window. Also, you can move and resize the window as needed.

✓ You can select how the contents of a folder are displayed. See Tasks 3, "Changing How the Contents of a Window Are Displayed," and 5, "Changing the View Style" later in this part.

1 ▶ Double-click the **My Computer** icon on the desktop.

2 ▶ Double-click the icon representing your hard drive (usually C:).

3 ▶ Each icon you see represents a folder on your hard drive. Double-click any of the folders.

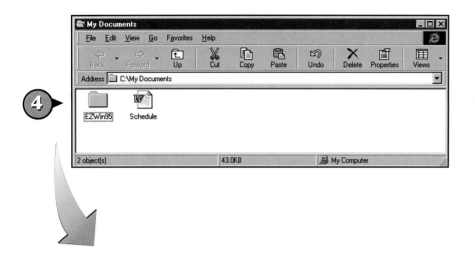

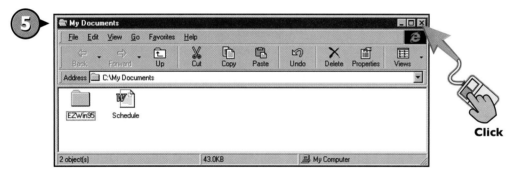

Click

4 Each folder icon represents groups of files and folders. Each document icon represents a document.

5 Click the **Close** button to close the window.

 To close a window and all its associated windows, hold down the **Shift** key and click the **Close** button.

Task 2: Editing a Document Using the Toolbar Buttons

Each window includes a toolbar that you can use to work with the documents and to change views of the folder contents.

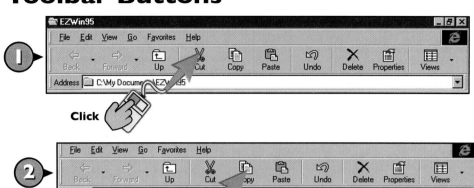

Click

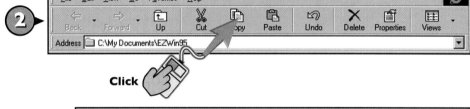

Click

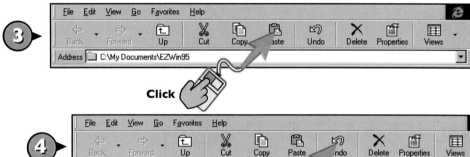

Click

✓ If you aren't sure what a toolbar button does, hover the mouse pointer over the button. A ToolTip containing the name of the button pops up.

Click

✓ You can use the buttons to move through your hard disk structure. Click the **Back** button to go back to a previously viewed page. Click the **Forward** button to go forward (after going back) to a previously viewed page. Click the **Up** button to display the next level up in the folder structure.

1 ▶ Click the **Cut** button to cut the selected item (file or folder).

2 ▶ Click the **Copy** button to copy the selected item.

3 ▶ Click the **Paste** button to paste the item you cut or copied.

4 ▶ Click the **Undo** button to undo the previous action.

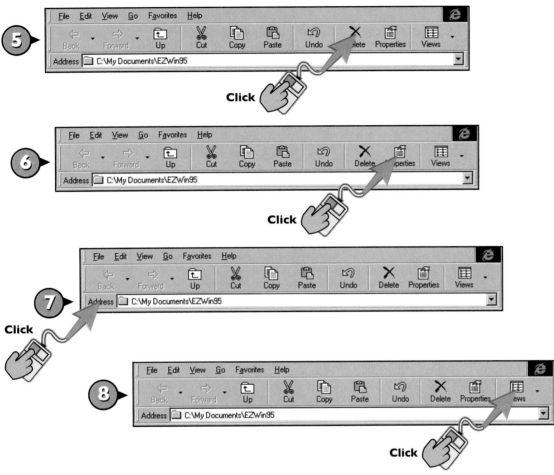

5. Click the **Delete** button to delete the selected item(s).

6. Click the **Properties** button to display the **Properties** dialog box with additional information about the selected item.

7. Click the **Address** button to select another folder or drive from the drop-down list.

8. Click the **Views** button to select a different view.

Task 3: Changing How the Contents of a Window Are Displayed

You can view the contents of a window in a variety of ways. By default, Windows uses large icons to display the contents of a window. If you want to see more of a window's contents at one time, you can change the view to **Small Icons**. You can also display such details about an item as its type, its size, and the date it was last modified. Changing the way a window displays its contents can make it easier to find what you need.

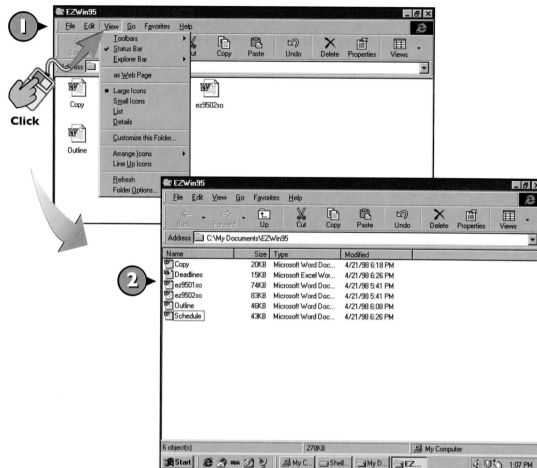

✓ The **View** command affects only the current window. Windows 95 will retain this view in that particular window until you make a change.

1 ▶ In the window you want to change, click the **View** menu and then choose the view you want.

2 ▶ The window displays the contents in that view (in this case, the **Details** view).

Task 4: Sorting the Contents of a Window

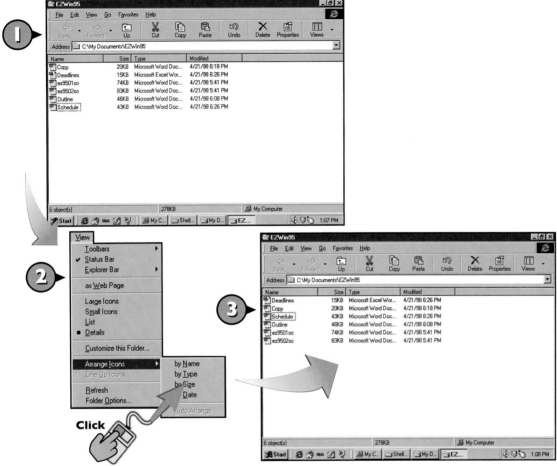

Click

You sort the contents of a window so that you can more easily find the files you want. Windows 95 enables you to arrange the contents by name, type, date, and size. Sorting the files is even easier if you choose to view them by the file details first. You can sort files viewed as large or small icons or as a list.

1. Open the window you want to sort and change to the view you want (in this case, the window is displayed in **Details** view).

2. Click **View**, choose the **Arrange Icons** command, and choose the sort order you want (in this case, **by Size**).

3. Windows sorts the files in the selected order. For instance, this view shows the files sorted by size from the smallest to the largest.

✓ You can also sort by name in alphabetical order, by file type, or by date from oldest to most recent by choosing the appropriate command from the **View | Arrange Icons** submenu. You can also click the column header in **Details** view to sort by that column.

✓ If you are working in the **My Computer** window, you have different options for arranging the icons. You can arrange by type, size, drive letter, or free space.

End Task

Task 5: Changing the View Style

If you have Internet Explorer 4 installed with Windows 95, you can select from different view styles for your folders. You can choose Web style to make browsing a file window similar to browsing a Web page. In Web style, you can single-click to open folders or files.

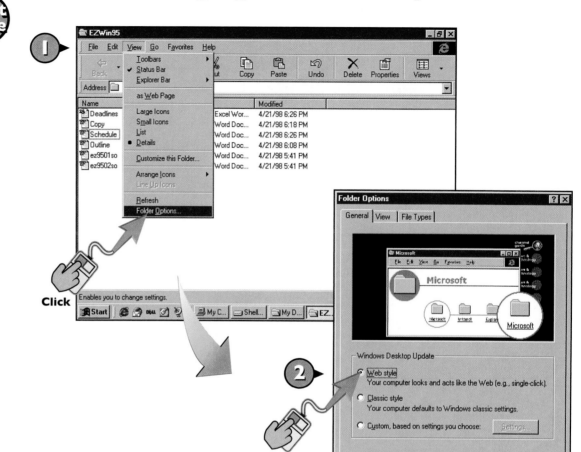

Click

Click

✓ To return to the Classic style, open the View menu and choose the Folder Options command. Choose Classic style and click the OK button.

✓ You can also choose custom settings by clicking the Custom radio button and then clicking the Settings button.

1 ▶ Click **View**, and then choose the **Folder Options** command.

2 ▶ Click the **Web style** radio button.

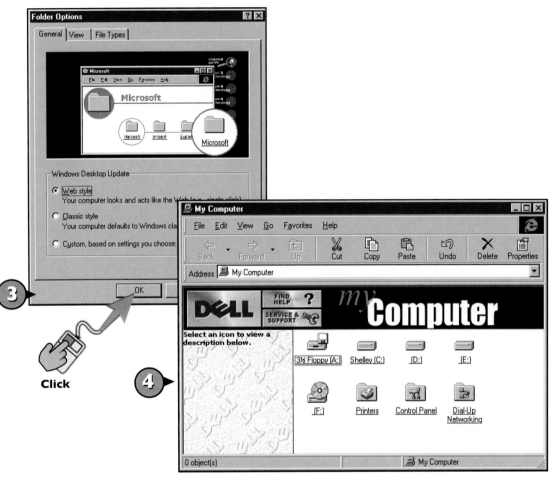

3 ▸ Click the **OK** button.

4 ▸ The contents of the window are displayed in **Web** view. You can simply click a folder or file to open it.

Task 6: Working in Web View

If you have Internet Explorer 4 installed with Windows 95, you can change to **Web** view. In this view style, you can single-click a folder or file to open it. The file windows resemble and operate like Web pages.

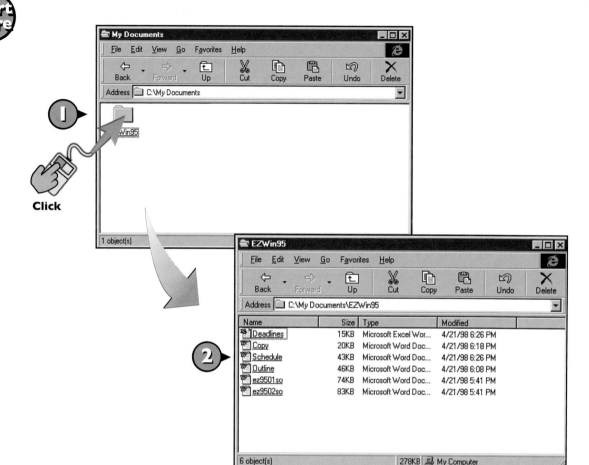

Click

✓ To return to the **Classic** style, open the **View** menu and choose the **Folder Options** command. Choose **Classic style** and click the **OK** button.

✓ For more information on browsing with Internet Explorer, see Part 9, "**Connecting to Online Services and the Internet.**"

1 ▶ Change to **Web** view, as covered in the preceding task, and click any of the folders in the window.

2 ▶ The contents of that folder are displayed.

Task 7: Creating a Folder

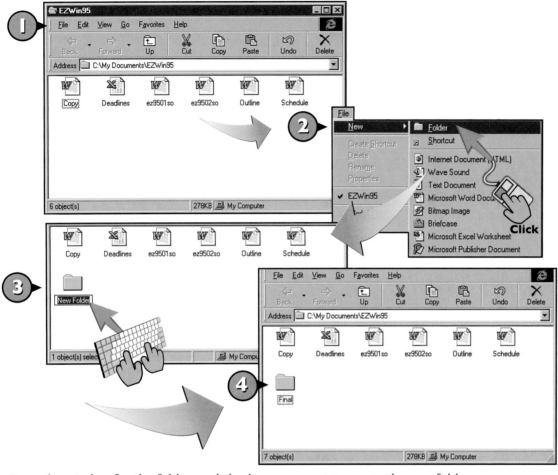

Working with your files is easier if you group related files into folders. For example, you might want to create a folder within your word-processing program's folder to hold all the documents you create with that program. Creating a folder enables you to keep your documents separated from the program's files so you can easily find your document files.

① Open the window for the folder or disk where you want to create the new folder.

② Click **File**, choose the **New** command, and then click **Folder**.

③ The new folder appears in the drive window, and the name is highlighted. To change the name of the folder, type a new name and press **Enter**.

④ The folder is added.

✓ If you change your mind about the new folder, you can always delete it. To delete the folder, select it and then press the **Delete** key on your keyboard. Click the **Yes** button to confirm the deletion.

✓ The folder name can contain as many as 255 characters, and can include spaces.

Task 8: Copying Folders

Windows 95 makes it easy for you to copy a folder and its contents and then paste them in a new location. You can, for example, copy a folder to a floppy disk to use as a backup or to move to another computer. In addition, you can copy a folder and its contents to another location on the hard drive if, for example, you want to revise the original file for a different use.

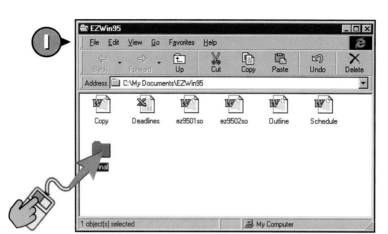

Click

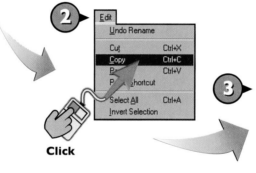

Click

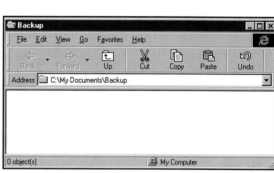

(✓) You can copy a folder by opening both the window that contains the folder (the source) and the window to which you want to copy the folder (the destination). Click the folder in the source window and drag it to the destination window.

(✓) You can also use the **Copy** button or right-click the folder and choose **Copy** from the shortcut menu.

1 ▶ Select the folder you want to copy.

2 ▶ Click **Edit**, and then choose the **Copy** command.

3 ▶ Open the folder or drive where you want to paste the copy.

Next Step

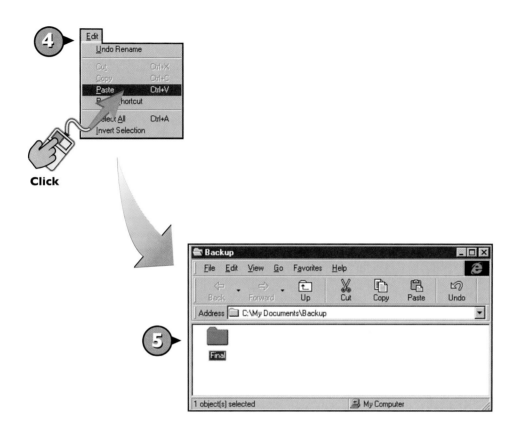

Click

④ ▶ Click **Edit**, and then choose the **Paste** command.

⑤ ▶ Windows copies the new folder and its contents to this location.

✓ **Keep in mind that you copy both the folder and its contents. If you don't need the copy, you can delete it. See Task 11, "Deleting Folders," for more information.**

Task 9: Moving Folders

Suppose, for example, that you want to move all related files and folders to the same place on your hard drive so you can find them quickly and easily. You can move a folder and its contents to another folder or to a disk so that you can reorganize your directory structure.

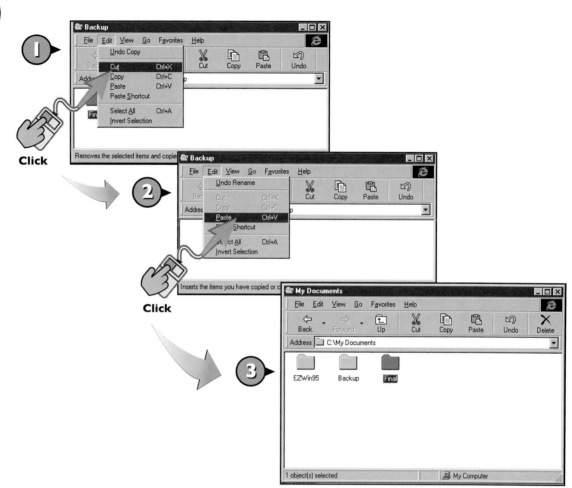

Start Here

Click

Click

✓ You can choose the **Undo** command from the **Edit** menu to undo the move if you change your mind.

✓ You can move a folder by opening both the window containing the folder (the source) and the window to which you will move the folder (the destination). Then press and hold the **Shift** key and drag the folder from the source window to the destination window.

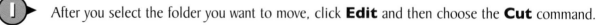

1 ▶ After you select the folder you want to move, click **Edit** and then choose the **Cut** command.

2 ▶ Open the drive or folder window where you want the folder to be moved. Click **Edit**, and then choose the **Paste** command.

3 ▶ Windows moves the folder to the new location.

End Task

Task 10: Renaming Folders

Start Here

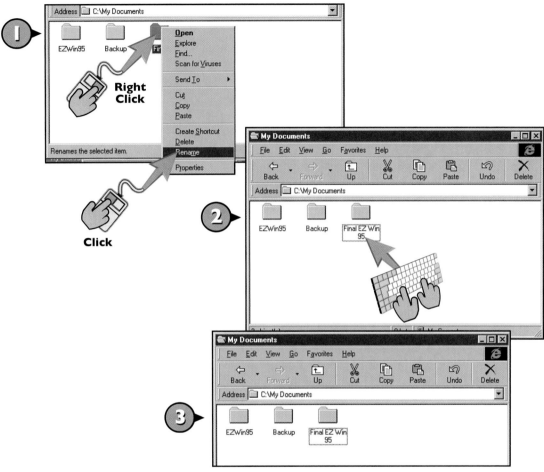

As you add more and more folders and files to your computer, you will eventually need to rearrange and reorganize them. If needed, you can change the names of folders—for instance, you can give a folder a more descriptive name.

① Right-click the folder you want to rename, and click the **Rename** command.

② Type a new name for the folder, and press **Enter**.

③ The folder is renamed.

✔ Folder names and filenames can contain as many as 255 characters, including spaces. You also can include letters, numbers, and other symbols on your keyboard, except the following:
| ? / : " * < > \

✔ Click the folder once to select it, and then single-click within the name to edit the name.

Task 11: Deleting Folders

You can delete folders when you no longer need them. When you delete a folder from your hard drive, you also delete its contents. Windows 95 places deleted folders in the **Recycle Bin**. You can restore deleted items from the **Recycle Bin** in case you realize you have placed items there by accident.

If you change your mind about deleting the folder, click the **No** button in the **Confirm Folder Delete** dialog box. Alternatively, you can undo the deletion by choosing the **Edit Undo** command. And finally, you can retrieve the item from the **Recycle Bin** (see Task 20, "Undeleting a File or Folder").

When you delete a folder from a floppy drive, that item is not placed in the **Recycle Bin**; it is immediately deleted from your system.

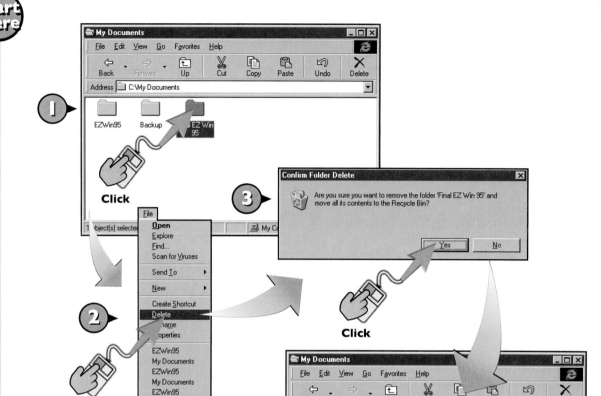

Select the folder you want to delete.

Click **File**, and then choose the **Delete** command.

Click the **Yes** button.

The folder is deleted.

Task 12: Selecting a Single File

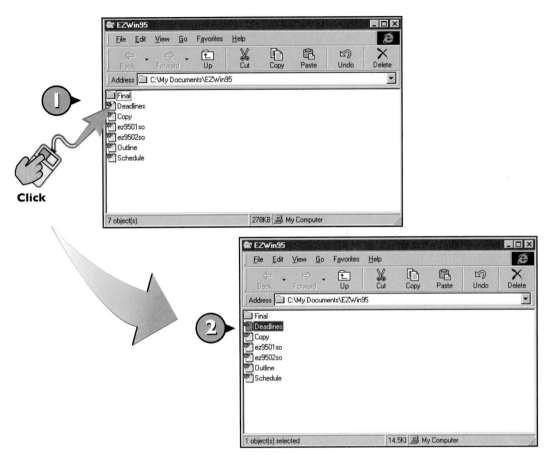

Click

When you want to work on files (copy, move, print, delete, and so on), you start by selecting the files you want. Selecting a single file is simple.

 Click the file you want to work with.

 That file is selected.

✓ **To deselect a file, click outside the selected file list.**

Task 13: Selecting Multiple Adjacent Files

Windows 95 enables you to easily select multiple files that are grouped together in the folder. Then you can work with this set of files— for instance, you can move, copy, print, or delete them.

Start Here

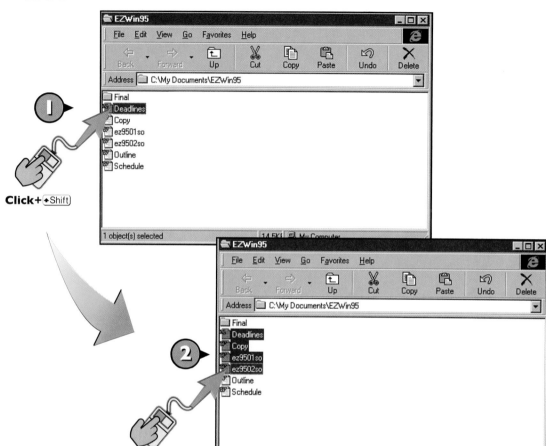

Click+▲Shift

Click+▲Shift

✓ Shift+clicking works differently in icon view. When you Shift+click in this view, all the files within the rectangular area from the first file to the last file are selected.

1 ▶ Click the first file of the group that you want to select, and then hold down the **Shift** key.

2 ▶ Click the last file in the group that you want to select; the first and last files, as well as all the files in between, are selected.

End Task

Task 14: Selecting Multiple Nonadjacent Files

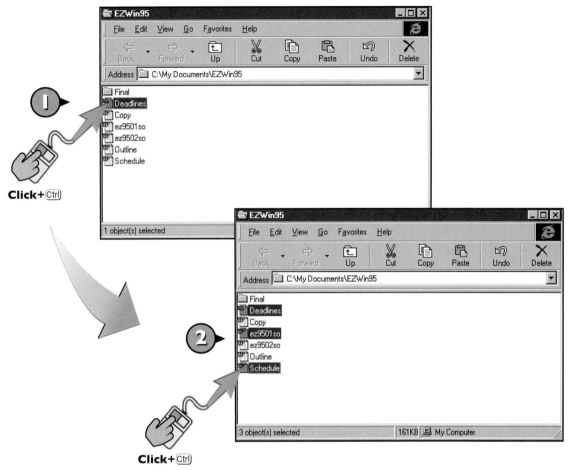

Click+ Ctrl

Click+ Ctrl

Even if the files you want to select are not grouped together, you can still select them using **Windows 95.** Once selected, you can then use any of the file commands to work on this set of selected items.

 Click the first file that you want to select, and hold down the **Ctrl** key.

 While holding down the **Ctrl** key, click each file that you want to select. Each file you click remains selected.

 To deselect a file, Ctrl+click it a second time.

Task 15: Selecting All Files

Windows 95 enables you to
select all the files in a
window. You might want to
do this to make a backup
copy of all the files in a
folder.

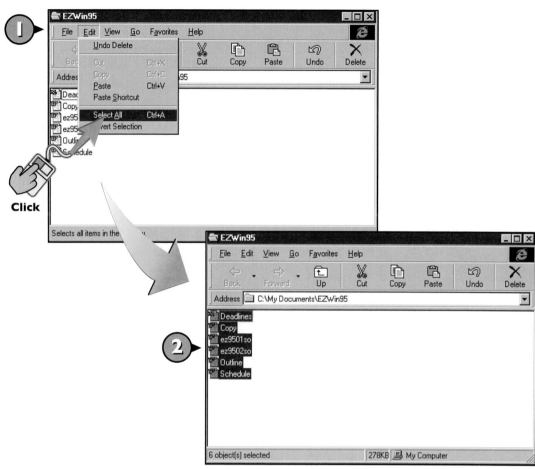

✓ To deselect all the files,
click outside any of the
selected files.

Click **Edit**, and then choose the **Select All** command.

All files are selected.

Task 16: Copying a File to Another Folder

Start Here

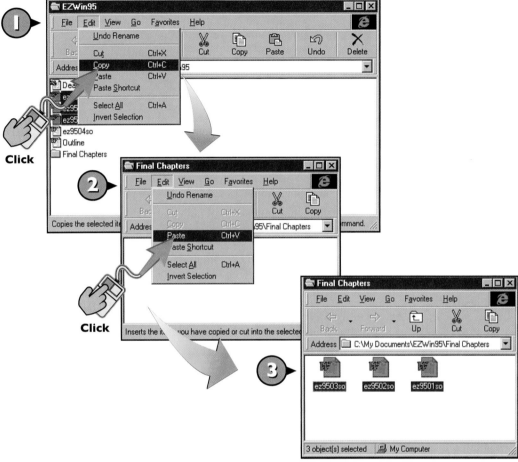

Click

Click

Windows makes it easy to copy files from one folder to another and from one disk to another. You might copy files in order to create a backup copy or to revise one copy while keeping the original file intact.

1 After you select the file(s) you want to copy, click **Edit**, and then choose the **Copy** command.

2 Open the folder to which you want to paste the copied file(s), click **Edit**, and then choose the **Paste** command.

3 Windows copies the file(s) to the new location.

✓ To use drag-and-drop to copy files, open the window that contains the file (source) and the window for the folder or drive to which you want to copy the file (destination). Hold the **Ctrl** key and drag the file to its destination.

✓ You can also click the **Copy** button or right-click and choose **Copy** from the shortcut menu.

End Task

Task 17: Copying a File to a Floppy Disk

You might want to copy a file to a floppy disk to take the file with you or to create a backup copy. Windows provides a shortcut (the **Send To** command) for copying a file to a floppy disk.

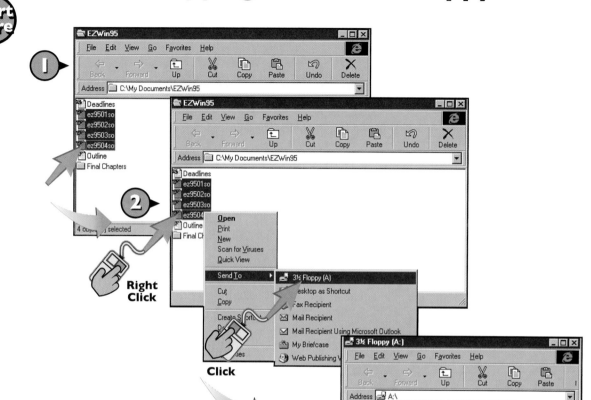

Right Click

Click

✓ If the disk is full, you see an error message. Insert a different disk and click the **Retry** button.

✓ You can also use the **Send To** command to send the file to the desktop as a shortcut (see Task 23, "Creating a Shortcut to a File or Folder").

 After you've inserted a disk into your floppy disk drive, select the file(s) you want to copy to the disk.

 Right-click the selected file(s). Choose the **Send To** command from the shortcut menu, and choose the appropriate floppy drive.

 The files are copied to that disk.

Task 18: Moving a File

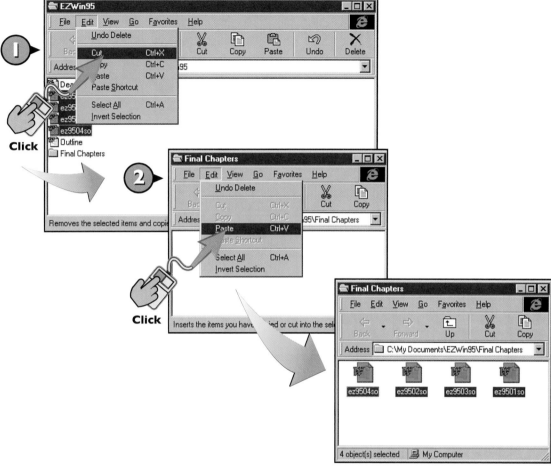

Click

Click

You might need to move files from one folder or drive to another (for example, in order to reorganize folders by putting similar files together in the same folder). You might also move a file that you accidentally saved in the wrong folder.

✓ If you make a mistake, you can undo the move by choosing the **Undo** command from the **Edit** menu.

✓ You can also drag a file to a different folder. Open the window that contains the file and the window for the folder or drive to which you want to move the file. If you are moving from one folder to another, simply drag the file(s) from one window to the other. If you are moving from one drive to another, hold down the **Shift** key and drag.

1 ▶ Select the file(s) you want to move, click **Edit**, and then choose the **Cut** command.

2 ▶ Open the folder or drive to which you want to paste the file(s), click **Edit**, and then choose the **Paste** command.

3 ▶ Windows moves the file(s) to the new location.

Task 19: Deleting a File

Eventually, your computer will become full of files, and you'll have a hard time organizing and storing them all. You can copy necessary files to floppy disks, tapes, and so on, and then delete the files from your hard drive to make room for new files. In addition, you will sometimes want to delete files you no longer need.

✓ You can undo a deletion by choosing the **Undo** command from the **Edit** menu. Alternatively, you can retrieve the deleted item from the **Recycle Bin**, as covered in the next task.

✓ Other alternatives for deleting files and folders include clicking the **Delete** button, right-clicking the folder or file and choosing **Delete** from the shortcut menu, and pressing the **Delete** key on your keyboard.

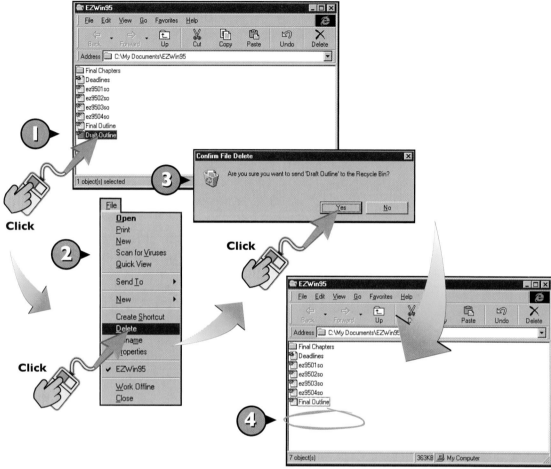

Click

Click

Click

Click

① Select the file(s) you want to delete.

② Click **File**, and then choose the **Delete** command.

③ Click **Yes** to delete the file(s).

④ Windows removes the file, placing it in the **Recycle Bin**.

End Task

Task 20: Undeleting a File or Folder

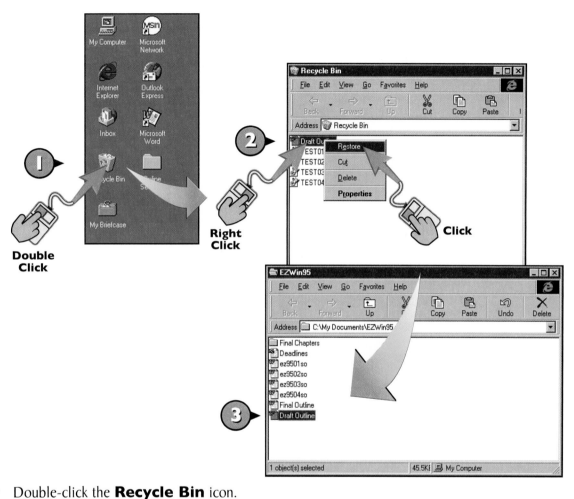

Sometimes you will delete a file or folder by mistake. You can retrieve the file or folder from the **Recycle Bin** (as long as the **Recycle Bin** has not been emptied) and return it to its original location.

Double Click

Right Click

Click

1. Double-click the **Recycle Bin** icon.

2. Select and then right-click the file(s) or folder(s) you want to undelete, and then choose the **Restore** command from the shortcut menu.

3. The file(s) or folder(s) is moved from the **Recycle Bin** to its original location.

If you want to be permanently rid of the files in the **Recycle Bin**, you can empty it. See the next task.

Task 21: Emptying the Recycle Bin

If you want to permanently delete items from your system, you need to empty the **Recycle Bin.** You should periodically empty the **Recycle Bin** also to save space; the files stored here take up disk space.

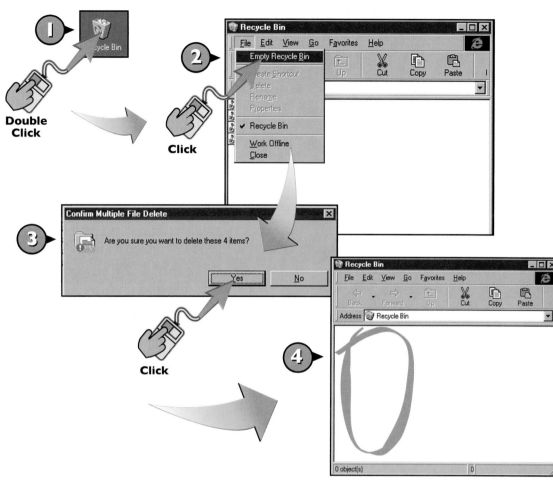

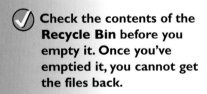

Check the contents of the **Recycle Bin** before you empty it. Once you've emptied it, you cannot get the files back.

1 Double-click the **Recycle Bin** icon.

2 After you make sure the **Recycle Bin** window doesn't contain anything you need to save, click **File** and then choose the **Empty Recycle Bin** command.

3 Click **Yes** to empty the **Recycle Bin**.

4 All the files and folders are removed.

Task 22: Displaying File or Folder Properties

Start Here

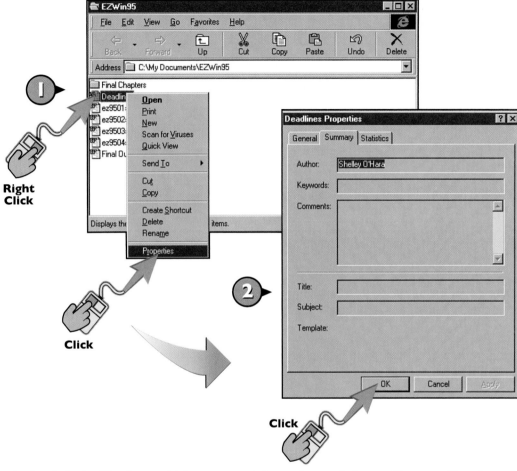

Right Click

Click

Click

Sometimes you may see a file or folder on your system and not know how it got there. What does the file contain? When was it added? You could get some information from **Details** view. As an alternative, you can display the properties for the file or folder.

Right-click the file about which you want information and choose **Properties** from the shortcut menu.

Review any of the information on the dialog box tabs, and then click the **OK** button.

✓ As a shortcut, you can also select the file or folder and then click the **Properties** button in the toolbar.

✓ Depending on the file type, you may see other tabs. Click each tab to view the relevant information.

End Task

Task 23: Creating a Shortcut to a File or Folder

If you often use the same file or folder, you might want fast access to it. If so, you can create a shortcut icon for the file or folder on the desktop. Double-clicking a shortcut icon to a file opens the file in the program you used to create the file. Double-clicking a folder displays the contents of the folder in a window.

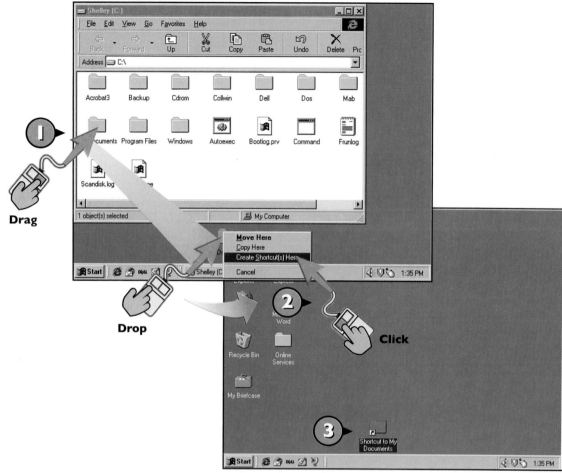

Drag

Drop

Click

✓ **Be sure to drag with the right mouse button. If you drag with the left, you move the file or folder.**

✓ **To delete the shortcut icon, right-click it and then choose Delete or drag the icon to the Recycle Bin.**

✓ **To rename the shortcut icon, right-click it and then choose Rename. Type a new name and press Enter.**

① Press and hold down the right mouse button and drag the folder or file icon to your desktop. Release the mouse button.

② When you release the mouse button, you see a pop-up menu. Choose the **Create Shortcut(s) Here** command.

③ Windows adds a shortcut icon to your desktop. (You can close the other windows to better see the shortcut icon, as I've done here).

End Task

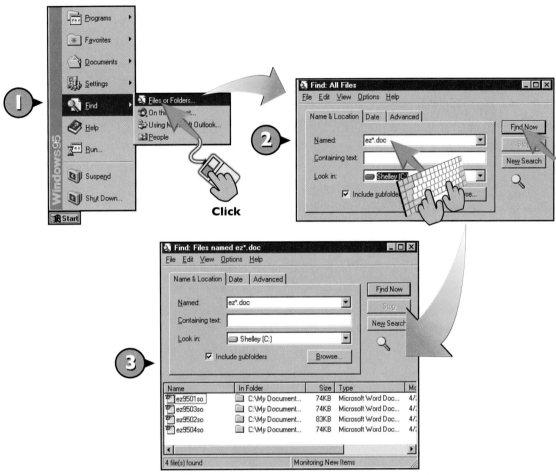

Click

After you've worked for months with your applications, your computer will become filled with various folders and files, which can make it nearly impossible for you to know where everything is. Luckily, Windows includes a command that helps you locate specific files or folders.

✓ You can use the characters ***** and **?** (known as *wildcards*) in the search. For example, to find all files ending with the extension **.doc**, you could type ***.doc**. Similarly, you could type **chap??.*** to find all files beginning with **chap**, followed by any two characters, and ending in any extension.

✓ If you do not know the name of the file but you know what type of file it is, click the **Advanced** tab in the **Find** dialog box. From the **Of type** list box, choose the type of file you're searching for. Click the **Find Now** button, and Windows performs the search.

1 ▶ Click the **Start** button, choose the **Find** command, and then choose **Files or Folders**.

2 ▶ Enter the name of the file you want to search for, and click the **Find Now** button.

3 ▶ Windows searches the hard drive by default, and displays a list of found files at the bottom of the dialog box.

Task 25: Finding Files and Folders by Contents

If you don't know the name of the file or folder you want, but you have some idea of what it contains, you can search for it by contents. Pick a unique word or phrase so that you don't end up with too many matches.

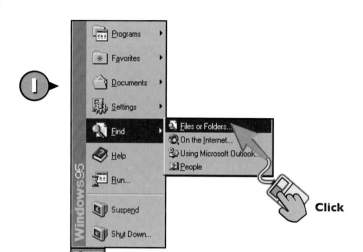

Click

✅ Windows will search the drive or folder you select and all subfolders. If you don't want the subfolders searched, uncheck the **Include subfolders** check box.

✅ You can search for more than one criterion. For example, if you enter a name and text, Windows searches for files that match both.

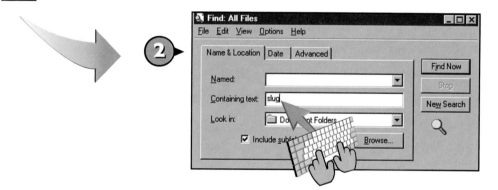

✅ Windows remembers the last search criteria you entered. To clear all the entries, click the **New Search** button and then confirm that you do want to clear the entries by clicking the **Yes** button.

1 Click the **Start** button, choose the **Find** command, and then choose **Files or Folders**.

2 Enter the text the file or folder contains.

Next Step

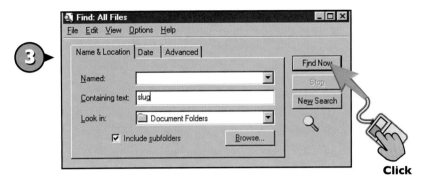

Click

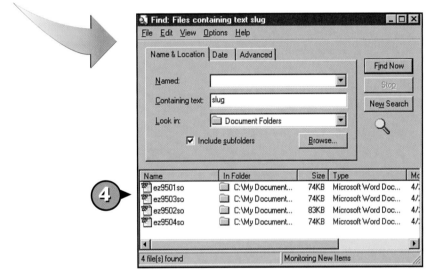

3 Click the **Find Now** button.

4 Windows searches the hard drive by default and displays a list of found files at the bottom of the dialog box.

✅ To change the drive on which Windows will conduct the search, display the **Look In** list box and choose the floppy or CD-ROM drive from the drop-down list.

✅ You can double-click any of the listed files to start the associated application and open that file or double-click any of the folders to display that folder.

Task 26: Finding Files and Folders by Date

As another search possibility, you can search for files within a particular date range. For instance, suppose you know you worked on a file this past week, but you can't remember the file's name. You can display a list of all files worked on within a certain date range.

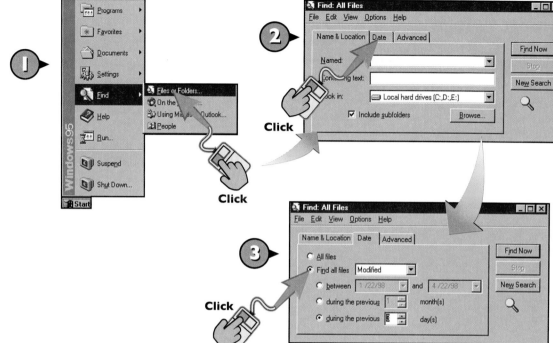

✓ You can select to find all files modified, accessed, or created within a certain date range. Click the **Find all files** drop-down list and select the match you want to make.

✓ You can select a date range between two specific dates or during the past number of months or days.

1 ► Click the **Start** button, choose the **Find** command, and then choose **Files or Folders**.

2 ► Click the **Date** tab.

3 ► Click the **Find all files** radio button to find all files modified, created, or accessed within the date range.

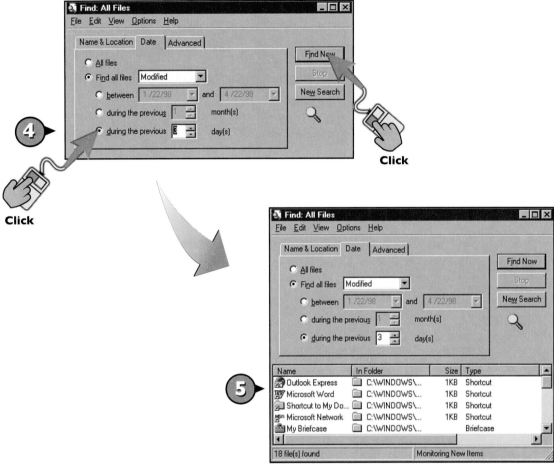

Click

Click

4 Select the date range, and then click the **Find Now** button.

5 Windows searches the hard drive by default and displays a list of found files at the bottom of the dialog box.

End Task

Task 27: Using Windows Explorer

You can use Windows Explorer in much the same way you use **My Computer**: to copy and move folders, to create and rename folders, to view details, and so on. You might be more comfortable using Explorer if you have used Windows 3.*x* because the Explorer in Windows 95 is very similar to the File Manager in previous versions of Windows. Alternatively, you might simply prefer the appearance of the Windows Explorer to that of the **My Computer** window.

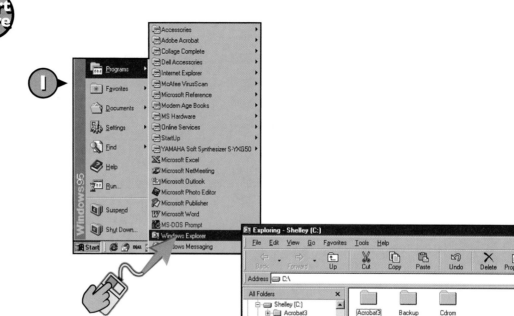

Click

Click

 You can use any of the commands and features of Windows Explorer to move, copy, delete, and work with files and folders. One thing that is easy to do with Explorer is to copy and move files by dragging.

1 ▶ Click the **Start** button, choose the **Programs** command, and choose **Windows Explorer**.

2 ▶ To display folders within a folder, click the plus sign.

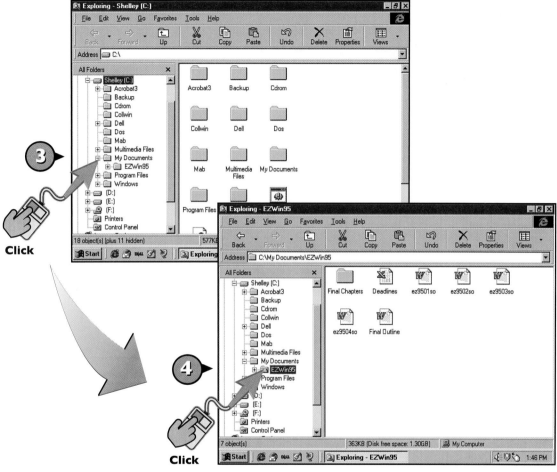

End
Task

Close Windows Explorer just as you do any other program: Choose the Exit command from the File menu or click the Close button in the program's title bar.

The left side of the split Explorer window lists all drives and folders on the hard drive. The right side displays the folders and files in the selected folder or drive on the left.

Any folder with a plus sign in front of it contains more folders and files.

3 ▶ The list expands to show other folders. A minus sign appears next to the folder name. To hide a folder, click the minus sign.

4 ▶ To display a folder's contents, click the folder in the list in the left pane. The folder's contents appear on the right side of the **Explorer** window.

Printing with Windows

All Windows applications use the same setup for your printer, which saves time and ensures that you can print from any Windows application without resetting for each program. When you first install Windows, it sets up your printer. If needed, you can set up more than one printer in Windows and choose the printer you want to use at any given time. In addition, you can easily manage printing for all of your applications through Windows.

You print a document from the application in which you created it. When you send a file to the printer, the file first goes to a *print queue*, or holding area. The print queue can contain one or many files at any time. While a file is in the print queue, you can pause, restart, and even cancel the printing. This part shows you how to control and manage printing in Windows.

Tasks

Task 1: Previewing a Document

In most applications, you can preview a document to check the margins, heads, graphics placement, and so on before you print. This gives you an overall idea of how the document will look on the page.

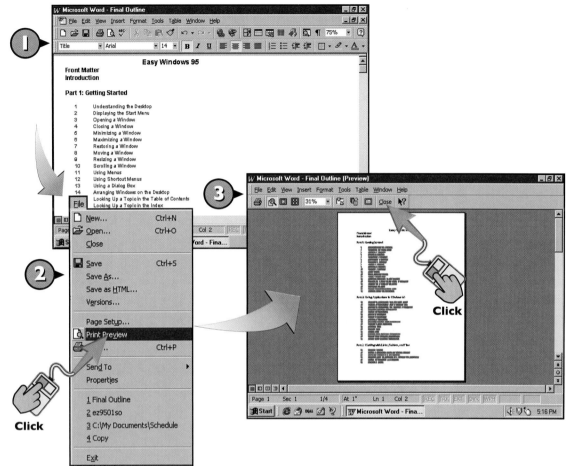

✓ The **Print Preview** view usually includes a toolbar for working with the document. Using buttons in this toolbar, you can magnify the view, print, change the margins, and more.

✓ Most programs have a preview option, but if you don't see this command listed in your program, it might not be available. You will have to print the document to see how it looks.

1 ▶ Open the document you want to print.

2 ▶ Click **File**, and choose the **Print Preview** command.

3 ▶ After you finish viewing the preview, click the **Close** button.

Task 2: Printing a Document

Start Here

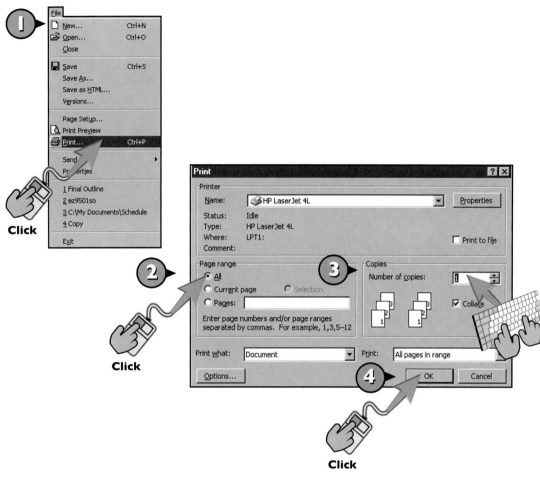

Click

Click

Click

You can print documents from any Windows 95 application. When you first install Windows, it sets up a primary printer, and you can print from any application using this printer. Printing your documents gives you a paper copy you can proofread, use in reports, give to coworkers, and so on.

✅ As a shortcut, look for a **Print** button in your toolbar. Alternatively, you can use a keyboard shortcut (usually **Ctrl+P**) to print.

✅ If nothing prints, make sure that your printer is plugged in, is online, and has paper.

✅ Each application's **Print** dialog box is slightly different, but they all work in basically the same way.

✅ To use a printer other than the default, choose the printer you want from the **Name** drop-down list in the **Print** dialog box.

① ▶ Click **File**, and then choose the **Print** command.

② ▶ Select a page range to print (the **All** radio button is selected by default).

③ ▶ Enter the number of copies to print.

④ ▶ Click the **OK** button.

End Task

Task 3: Viewing the Print Queue

Start Here

The print queue lists the documents that have been sent to a printer, and shows how far along the printing is. Using the print queue, you can pause, restart, or cancel print jobs. This task shows how to view the print queue.

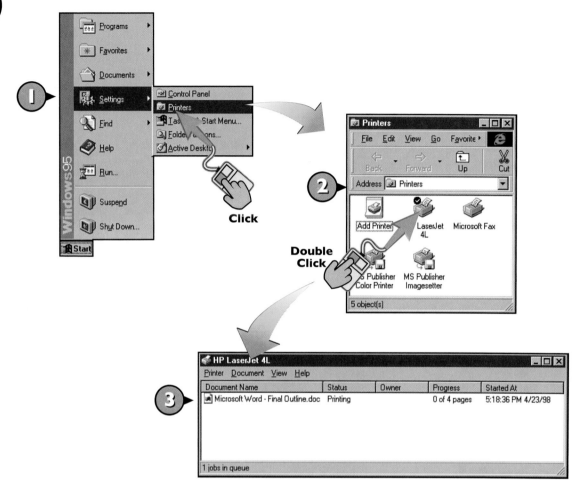

Click

Double Click

To close the print queue, click the **Close** button.

You can also display the print queue by double-clicking the **Printer** icon in the taskbar. This icon appears whenever you are printing something.

If the print queue window is empty, it means there is nothing in the print queue.

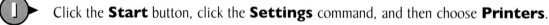

1 ▶ Click the **Start** button, click the **Settings** command, and then choose **Printers**.

2 ▶ Double-click the printer whose print queue you want to view.

3 ▶ The printer window displays a list of the documents in the queue, as well as statistics about the documents being printed.

Task 4: Pausing and Restarting the Printer

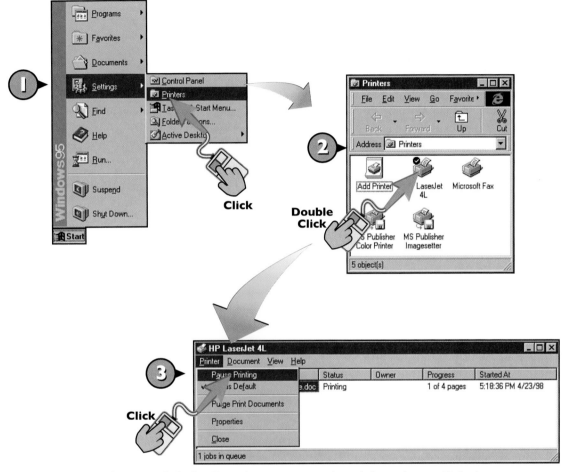

You might want to pause printing if, for example, you have a change to make in the text or you want to load a different paper type. You can easily pause the printing from the **Printers** folder, and you can restart it at any time.

✓ You have to be quick to pause or stop a short print job. If nothing appears in the print queue, it probably means that the entire print job has already been sent to the printer.

✓ You can use the **Document** menu in the print queue to pause printing on a specific job (if, for example, you have sent several jobs to the printer but want to pause for a particular job). Select the job you want to pause and choose the **Pause Printing** command from the **Document** menu.

✓ To restart the printer after you have paused it, click **Printer** and then click the **Pause Printing** command again.

① ▶ Click the **Start** button, click the **Settings** command, and then choose **Printers**.

② ▶ Double-click the printer whose print queue you want to view.

③ ▶ Click **Printer**, and then choose the **Pause Printing** command.

Task 5: Canceling Printing

If you discover an error in the job you are printing, or if you decide that you need to add something to it, you can cancel the print job. Canceling the print job prevents you from wasting time and paper.

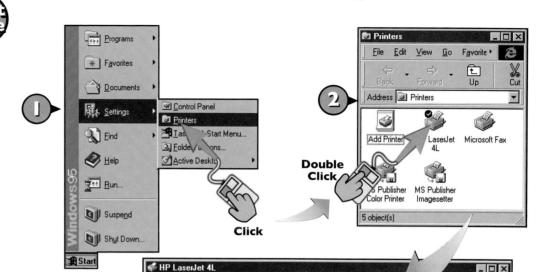

✓ Depending on your computer and your printer, the print job might be listed in the print queue for only a few seconds before it is sent to the printer. You might not be able to cancel it.

 Click the **Start** button, click the **Settings** command, and then choose **Printers**.

 Double-click the printer whose print queue you want to view.

 In the print queue, select the print job you want to cancel.

 Click **Document**, and then choose the **Cancel Printing** command.

Task 6: Setting the Default Printer

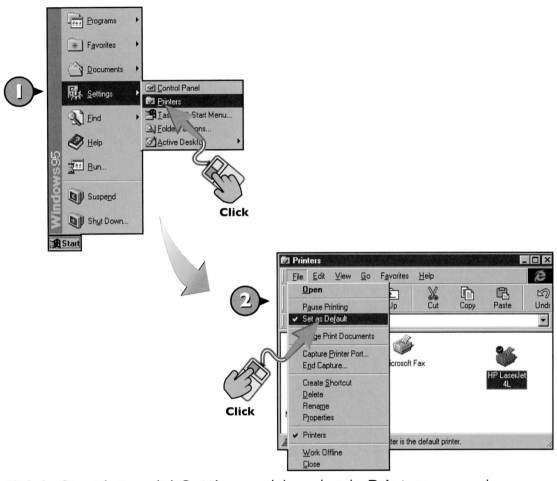

Click

Click

If you have more than one printer connected, you must select one as the default. The default printer you set in Windows is the printer your applications automatically use when you choose to print. The default printer is the one you want most of your documents printed on.

1. Click the **Start** button, click **Settings**, and then select the **Printers** command.

2. After you select the printer you want to choose as the default, click **File**, and then choose the **Set as Default** command.

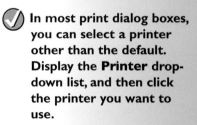 In most print dialog boxes, you can select a printer other than the default. Display the **Printer** drop-down list, and then click the printer you want to use.

Task 7: Changing Printer Settings

You can change printer settings, such as the port, driver, and job priority, as well as other settings specific to your printer. You might, for example, switch to a new printer driver so that your printer works better with your applications; alternatively, you might change the port to which your printer connects to make room for another external device, such as a modem or tape drive.

Dithering blends colors into patterns for smoother printing. Black and white is blended into gray. You can choose from various options to show sharp edges (**Line Art**) or smooth edges (**Fine**). Choose **Vector Graphics** to speed up printing but create less-detailed images; choose **Raster Graphics** to sharpen overlaid colors and details. Specify the intensity to tell Windows how dark or light to print the graphics.

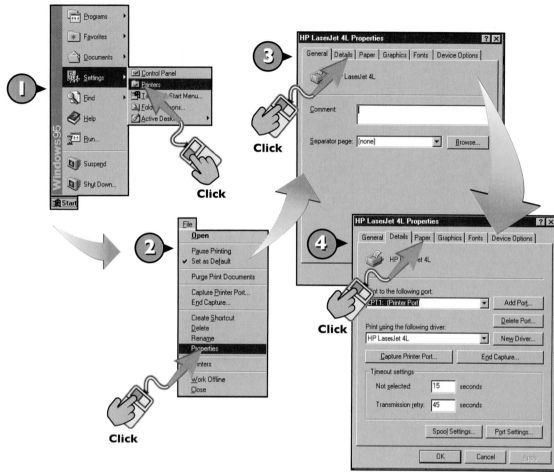

1. Click the **Start** button, click the **Settings** command, and then choose **Printers**.

2. After you select the printer you want to modify, click **File**, and then choose the **Properties** command.

3. Click the **Details** tab.

4. Make the necessary changes to the printer port, driver, timeout settings, and so on. After you finish, click the **Paper** tab.

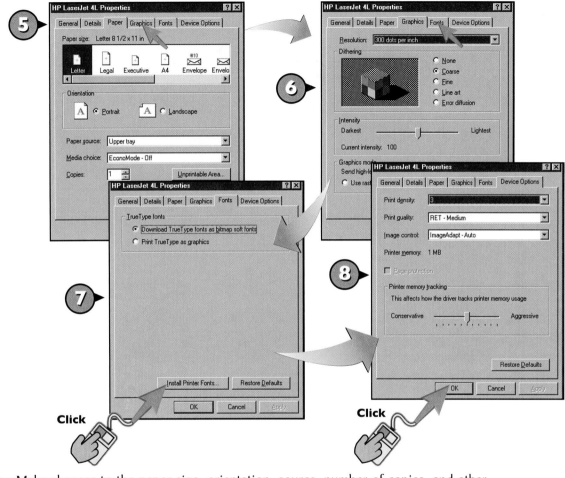

5 Make changes to the paper size, orientation, source, number of copies, and other options. After you finish, click the **Graphics** tab.

6 Make changes to the print resolution, dithering, shading intensity, and graphics mode. After you finish, click the **Fonts** tab.

7 Install any printer fonts or new font cartridges. Choose any font cartridge you have added to enable the use of its fonts in Windows. After you finish, click the **Device Options** tab.

8 Choose printed text quality (the available options depend on your printer). After you finish, click the **OK** button.

✅ Changing the printer's properties changes them for all documents you print on that printer. If you want to change properties for just one document, use the **Page Settings** or **Print Setup** command in the particular program.

✅ If you make a change in the **Paper, Graphics, Fonts,** or **Device Options** tab and change your mind about the changes, you can click the **Restore Defaults** button to cancel the changes.

✅ The number and title of tab settings in the **Properties** dialog will vary depending on the type of printer you have.

✅ Timeout settings specify how long Windows will wait before reporting an error to you.

Task 8: Adding a Printer

You can add a new printer to your Windows setup using a step-by-step guide called a *wizard* that Windows provides. Use the wizard any time you get a new printer or change printers.

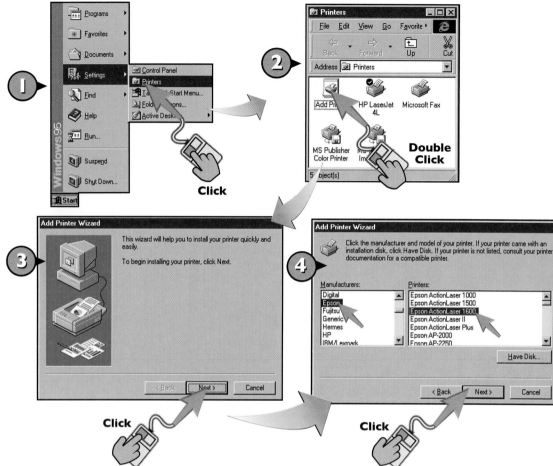

✓ You can cancel this process at any time by clicking the **Cancel** button in any of the wizard dialog boxes.

✓ Click the **Back** button in a wizard dialog box to return to the previous dialog and review or modify your selections.

1 ▶ Click the **Start** button, click the **Settings** command, and then choose **Printers**.

2 ▶ Double-click the **Add Printer** icon.

3 ▶ Click the **Next** button to continue with the installation.

4 ▶ Select the name of your printer's manufacturer from the **Manufacturers** list box, select the appropriate printer from the **Printers** list box, and then click **Next**.

Next Step

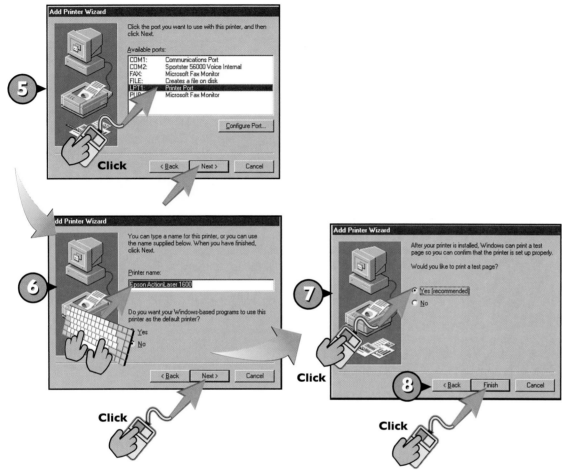

Click

Click

Click

Click

5 ▸ Select the appropriate port, and then click **Next**.

6 ▸ Enter a name for the printer (or accept the one Windows has given it), and then select whether you want the new printer to be the default printer. After you finish, click **Next**.

7 ▸ Click the **Yes** radio button to print a test page.

8 ▸ Click the **Finish** button. Windows adds the new printer's icon to the **Printers** folder.

If you want to use drivers supplied by your printer manufacturer, click the **Have Disk** button instead of clicking **Next**. Insert the appropriate disk and follow the onscreen instructions.

If you select **Yes** to print a test page, Windows prints a test page, and you are asked whether it printed successfully. Answer the prompt and then continue the setup.

End Task

Task 9: Deleting a Printer

If you get a new printer, you can delete the setup for the old printer so that you don't get confused about which printer is which. Deleting a printer removes it from the available list of printers.

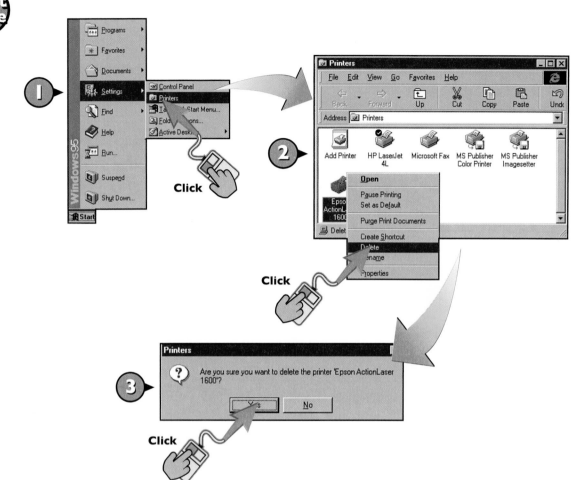

Start Here

Click

Click

Click

✓ If you delete a printer by mistake, you can always add it back using the **Add Printer** wizard (refer to the preceding task).

1 ▶ Click the **Start** button, click the **Settings** command, and then click **Printers**.

2 ▶ Right-click the printer you want to delete, and choose the **Delete** command from the shortcut menu.

3 ▶ Click the **Yes** button to confirm the deletion.

Task 10: Adding a Printer Icon on the Desktop

Start Here

For fast access to your printer, you can add a printer icon to your desktop. You can then double-click this icon to view the print queue. You can also drag documents from a file window to the printer icon to print the documents.

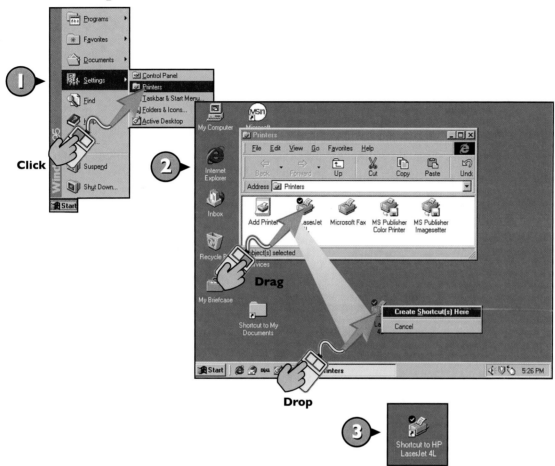

Click

Drag

Drop

If you drag with the left mouse button, you see a message telling you that you cannot copy the icon to the desktop. You are asked whether you want to create a shortcut icon instead. Click the **Yes** button to create a shortcut icon.

1 ▶ Click the **Start** button, click the **Settings** command, and then select **Printers**.

2 ▶ With the right mouse button, drag your printer icon from the **Printer** folder to your desktop, and then click the **Create Shortcut(s) Here** command.

3 ▶ The printer shortcut is added to your desktop.

To delete the shortcut icon, right-click it and then select **Delete** from the shortcut menu. When prompted to confirm the deletion, click the **Yes** button.

Personalizing Windows

To make Windows most suited to how you work, Microsoft has made it easy for you to customize the program. You can move and resize the taskbar, placing it where you like on the desktop. You can adjust the colors used for onscreen elements such as the title bar. You can change how the mouse works, when sounds are played, and more. Windows 95 includes many options for setting up your work environment just the way you want. This part shows you how to customize Windows.

Tasks

Task 1: Showing and Hiding the Taskbar

Windows' default is to show the taskbar at all times on the desktop. You can, however, hide the taskbar so that you have more room on the desktop for other windows, folders, and programs. When you hide the taskbar, it disappears while you are working in a window and then reappears when you move the mouse to the bottom of the screen.

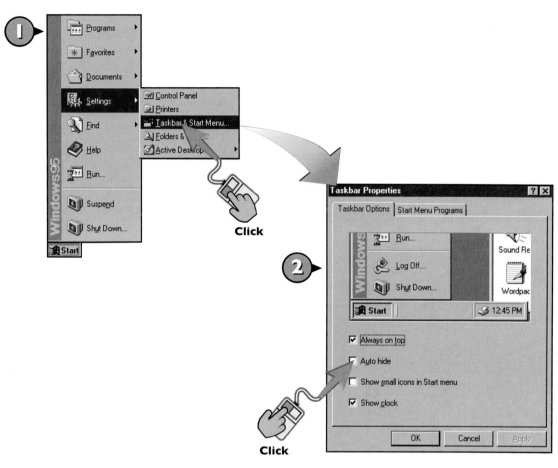

Click

Click

✓ To undo this change, open the **Start** menu, click the **Settings** command, and then click the **Taskbar & Start Menu** command. Click the **Auto Hide** option to remove the check mark, and then click **OK**.

✓ You can right-click a blank area of the taskbar and select **Properties** to make a change.

1 ▸ Click **Start**, click the **Settings** command, and then select **Taskbar & Start Menu**.

2 ▸ Click the **Auto hide** check box.

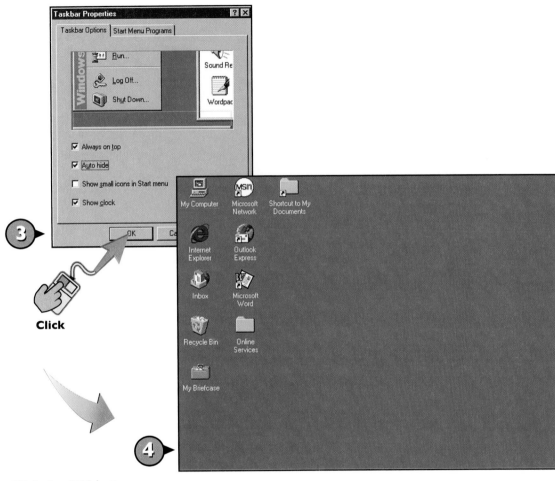

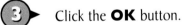

3 Click the **OK** button.

4 The dialog box closes, and the taskbar disappears.

Task 2: Moving the Taskbar

Windows enables you to place the taskbar in the top, left, right, or bottom of the screen so that the desktop is set up how you like it. Try moving the taskbar to various areas on the screen, and then choose the area you like best.

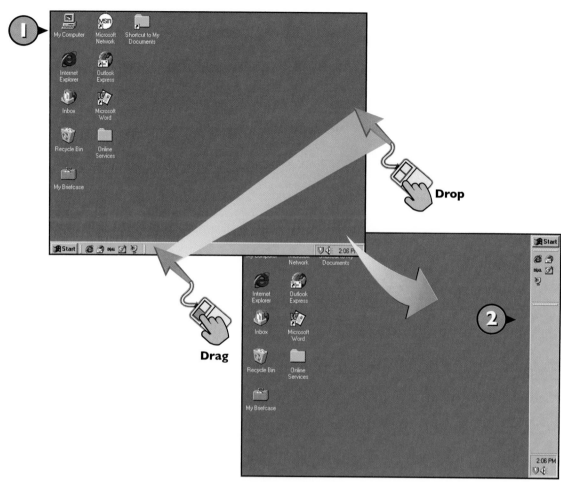

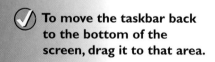 To move the taskbar back to the bottom of the screen, drag it to that area.

 Position the mouse pointer over a blank area on the taskbar. Press and hold the left mouse button and drag the taskbar to the location you want.

 When you release the mouse button, the taskbar jumps to the new location.

Task 3: Resizing the Taskbar

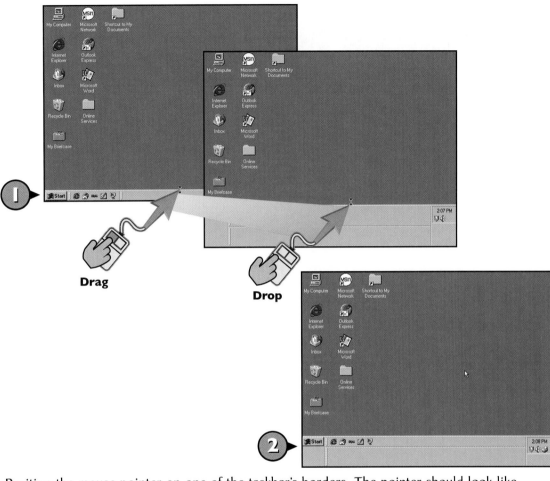

Drag

Drop

In addition to moving the taskbar, you can also resize it (for example, making it larger so that the buttons are bigger and easier to read). You resize the taskbar just as you resize a window—by dragging its border.

✓ You can select to display small icons and to enable or disable the clock in the taskbar. Click **Start**, choose **Settings**, and then choose **Taskbar & Start Menu.** Then check or uncheck **Show small icons in Start menu** and **Show clock.**

① Position the mouse pointer on one of the taskbar's borders. The pointer should look like a double-headed arrow. Drag the arrow to resize the taskbar.

② After you release the mouse button, the taskbar is resized.

Task 4: Using Wallpaper for the Desktop

You can personalize your desktop in Windows by adding wallpaper. Windows offers many colorful wallpaper options, including cars, honeycombs, squares, zigzags, and more.

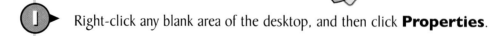

Click

Click

You can also add a pattern to the desktop, as covered in the next task.

*If you see only one small image in the center of your screen after selecting a wallpaper, click the **Display** drop-down list and choose **Tile**. Click **Apply**, and then click **OK** to accept the changes.*

*To revert to a plain background, follow these steps, but select **(None)** from the **Wallpaper** list.*

1 Right-click any blank area of the desktop, and then click **Properties**.

2 Select the wallpaper you want displayed on your desktop. The selected wallpaper appears on the sample monitor.

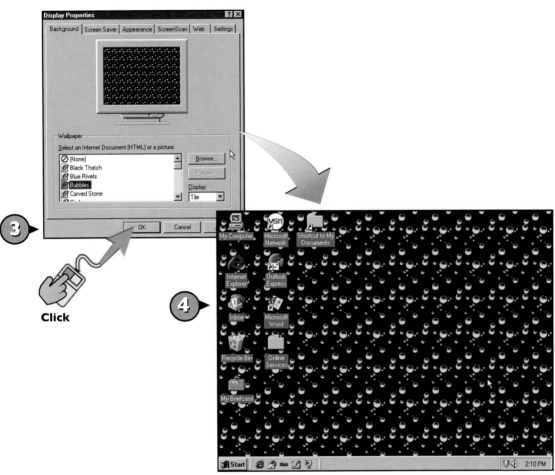

Click

<table>
<tr><td>**3**</td><td>Click the **OK** button.</td></tr>
</table>

<table>
<tr><td>**4**</td><td>The wallpaper is added to your desktop background.</td></tr>
</table>

Task 5: Using a Pattern for the Desktop

If you don't like the wallpaper selections, you might want to experiment with a pattern. Windows offers paisley, tulip, waffle, and box background patterns (among others).

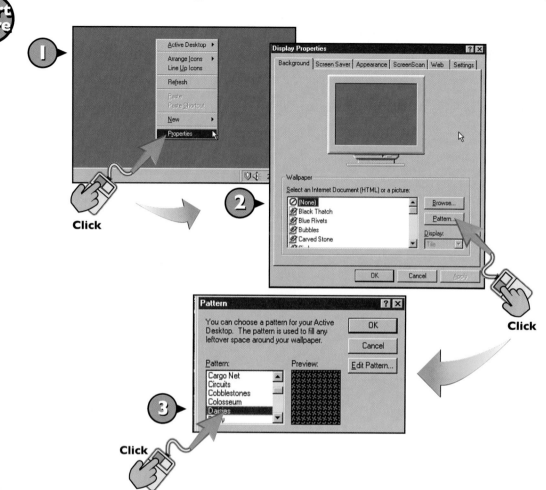

✓ Using wallpaper and patterns generally slows the speed of your computer and taxes its memory. If your applications seem too slow or if you decide you don't want a pattern or wallpaper, return to the **Display Properties** dialog box, click the **Patterns** button, and choose **(None)**.

✓ A pattern is a usually a small, repeating image. Wallpaper is usually one big image, like a picture.

1 ▶ Right-click any blank area of the desktop, and then click **Properties**.

2 ▶ Click the **Pattern** button.

3 ▶ Select the pattern you want displayed on your desktop. The selected pattern appears in the **Preview** area.

Next Step

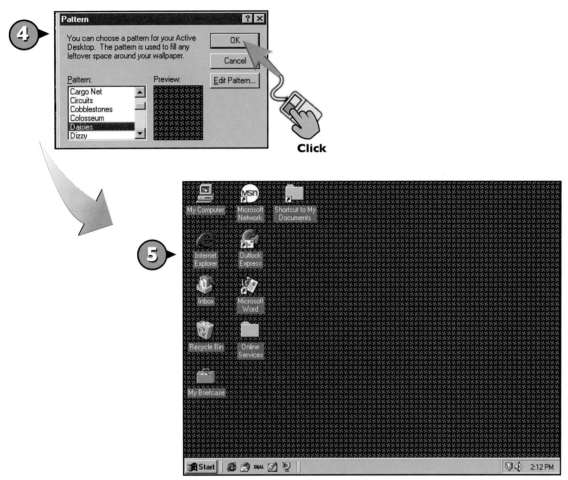

Click

 Click the **OK** button to use this pattern and to close the **Pattern** dialog box.

 Windows uses the selected pattern on your desktop.

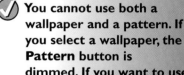 You cannot use both a wallpaper and a pattern. If you select a wallpaper, the **Pattern** button is dimmed. If you want to use a pattern, select **(None)** from the **Wallpaper** list.

Task 6: Changing the Colors Windows Uses

Windows enables you to change the sets of colors used for certain onscreen elements such as the title bar, background, and so on. These sets of colors are called *schemes*, and you can select colors that work best for you and your monitor. Lighter colors might, for example, make working in some Windows applications easier on your eyes. On the other hand, you might prefer bright and lively colors.

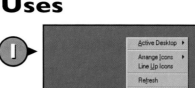

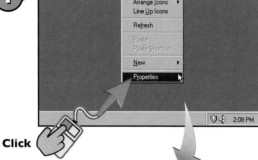

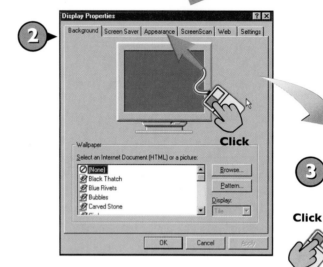

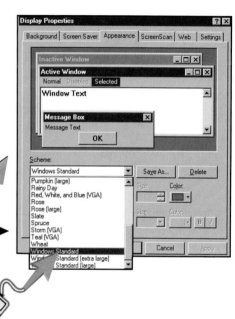

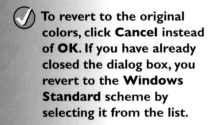 To revert to the original colors, click **Cancel** instead of **OK**. If you have already closed the dialog box, you revert to the **Windows Standard** scheme by selecting it from the list.

 Right-click any blank area of the desktop, and then click **Properties**.

 Click the **Appearance** tab.

 From the **Scheme** drop-down list, select any of the available schemes.

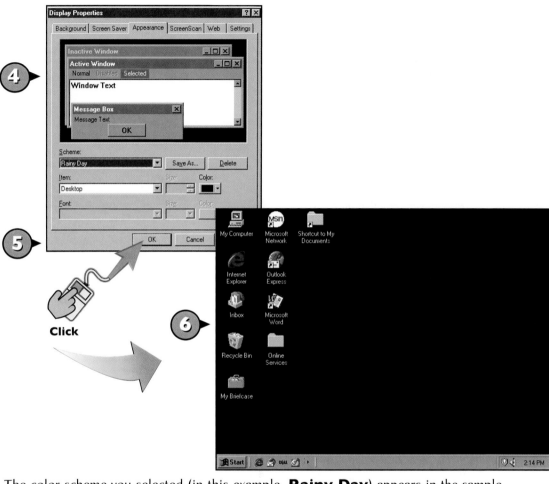

Click

4 ► The color scheme you selected (in this example, **Rainy Day**) appears in the sample box.

5 ► Click the **OK** button to accept the changes.

6 ► Windows uses the new set of colors you selected.

When you see a preview of the color scheme, you can change any individual item's color by clicking the item and then selecting a different color from the **Color** list. When you're satisfied with your changes, click **OK** to accept the changes.

End Task

Task 7: Using a Screen Saver

On older monitors, colors would, over time, burn into the screen, and you would see a "ghost" of the Windows screen on your display after you turned off your computer. A screen saver (a moving pattern of dark and light colors or images) helped protect your screen by displaying a pattern whenever the computer was on but inactive. These days, monitor burn-in isn't a problem, and screen savers are used mostly for fun.

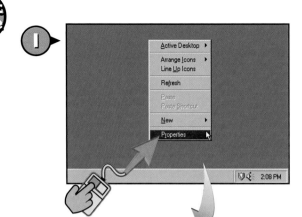

Click

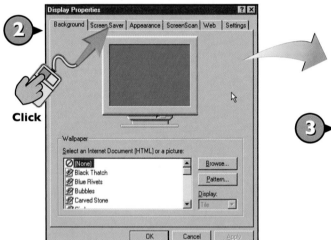

Click

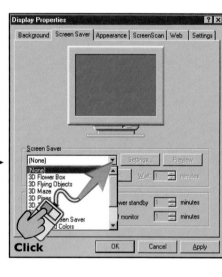

Click

If you want to see what the screen saver will look like when it is displayed on the full screen, click the **Preview** button. Click the mouse button or press the spacebar to return to the **Display Properties** dialog box.

1 ▶ Right-click any blank area of the desktop, and then click **Properties**.

2 ▶ Click the **Screen Saver** tab.

3 ▶ Click the **Screen Saver** drop-down list box arrow to display the list of available screen savers, and then select the screen saver you want to use.

Next Step

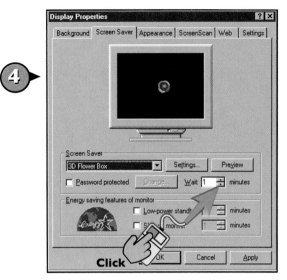

Click

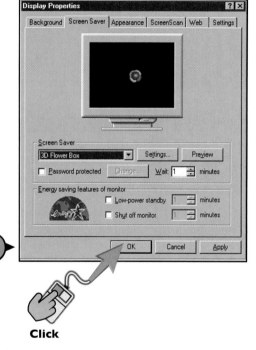

Click

The screen saver you selected appears on the sample monitor. Enter the number of minutes you want Windows to wait before it starts the screen saver in the **Wait** text box.

Click the **OK** button.

✓ Click the **Settings** button to select options for how the screen saver is displayed; these options vary depending on the screen saver. Make your choices and click the **OK** button.

✓ When the screen saver is displayed, move the mouse or press the spacebar to return to the normal view.

✓ To turn off the screen saver, open the **Display Properties** dialog box, click the **Screen Saver** tab, and select **None**. Click the **OK** button.

Task 8: Saving Energy

To save energy, you can have Windows turn off your monitor or switch your monitor to standby mode. You can find these options on the **Screen Saver** tab.

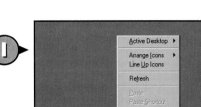

Start Here

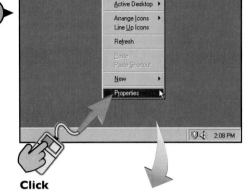

Click

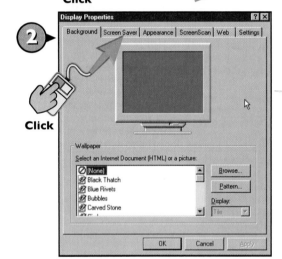

Click

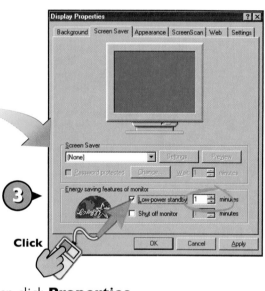

Click

✓ If these options are not available (are dimmed), your monitor does not support energy saving features.

✓ Your monitor might have other options (like the ScreenScan option shown in these figures). Look for other tabs in the **Display Properties** dialog box and check the documentation that came with your monitor.

1 ▶ Right-click any blank area of the desktop, and then click **Properties**.

2 ▶ Click the **Screen Saver** tab.

3 ▶ To turn on standby mode, check the **Low-power standby** check box and then enter the number of minutes to wait.

Next Step

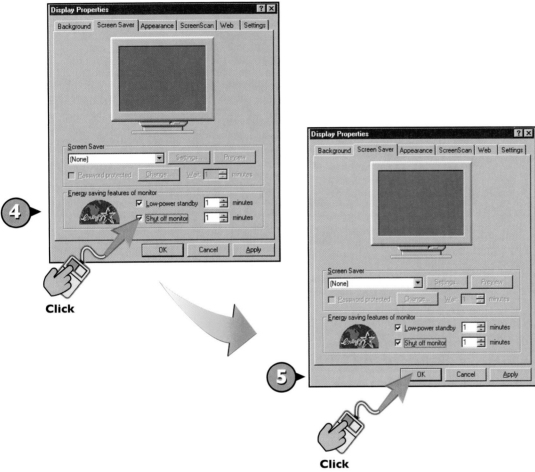

Click

Click

④ To shut off the monitor after a certain idle period, check **Shut off monitor** and then enter the number of minutes to wait.

⑤ Click the **OK** button.

Many monitors enable you to select certain options about how they operate—such as the number of colors they display or their resolution (*resolution* measures the number of pixels or picture elements displayed. An example of a common resolution is 800×600). You might need to change your monitor's display properties if you get a new monitor, want to update your monitor driver, or want to change how the monitor looks.

Task 9: Changing How Your Monitor Works

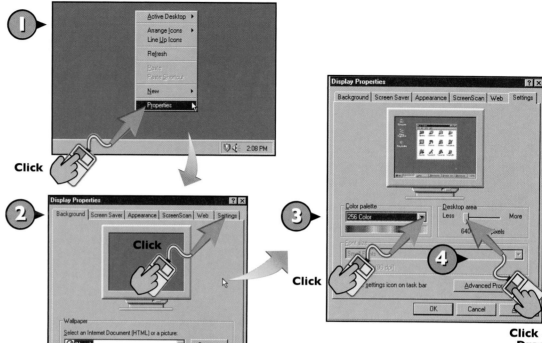

Click

Click

Click

Click & Drag

To upgrade a monitor or adapter, click the **Advanced** button on the **Settings** tab, and then select either the **Adapter** or **Monitor** tab. Click the **Change** button and follow the wizard's instructions for installing a new monitor or adapter.

 Right-click any blank area of the desktop, and then click **Properties**.

 Click the **Settings** tab.

 To change the number of colors used, display the **Colors** drop-down list and choose the number you want.

 To change the resolution, drag the **Screen area** bar to the desired setting.

Next Step

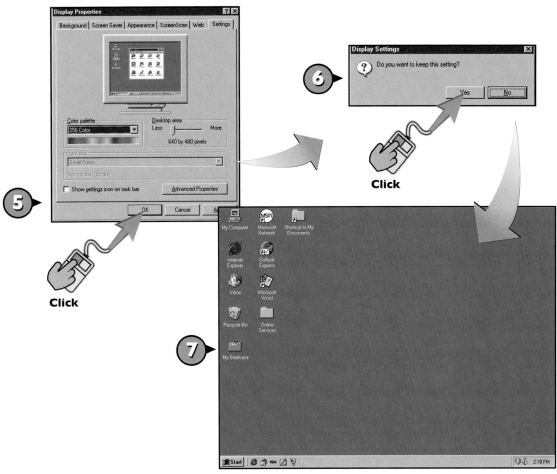

Click

Click

5 Click the **OK** button.

6 When prompted whether you want to keep the settings, click the **Yes** button. Click **OK** to close the dialog box.

7 Windows uses the new settings—here a desktop area of 800×600.

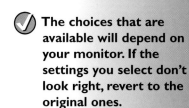

The choices that are available will depend on your monitor. If the settings you select don't look right, revert to the original ones.

End Task

If you have used the Internet, you might be comfortable with the methods used on it for viewing content. For example, when you browse the Internet, you can click a link to display its contents. You can set up your desktop to browse its contents just like a Web page if you have Internet Explorer 4. You also can display Web channels, which you can use to browse the Internet. (For more information about browsing the Internet, see Part 9, "Connecting to Online Services and the Internet.")

Task 10: Viewing the Desktop as a Web Page

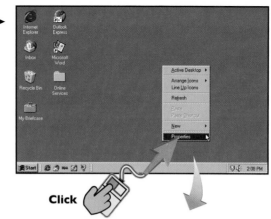

Click

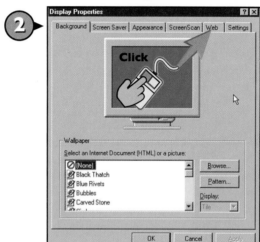

Click

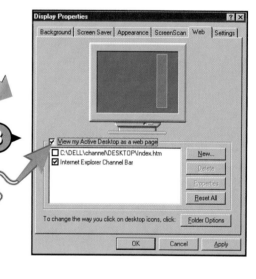

Click

✓ To revert to the regular desktop, right-click a blank area of the desktop, choose **Active Desktop**, and click **View As Web Page** to deselect this option.

 Right-click any blank area of the desktop, and then click **Properties**.

 Click the **Web** tab.

 Check the **View my Active Desktop as a web page** check box.

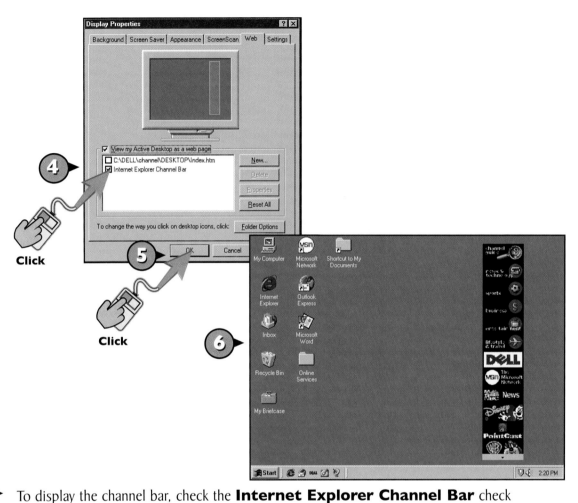

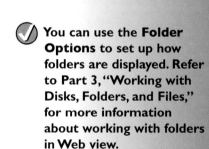

You can use the **Folder Options** to set up how folders are displayed. Refer to Part 3, "Working with Disks, Folders, and Files," for more information about working with folders in Web view.

You can also click the **Start** button, select the **Settings** option, click **Active Desktop**, and select **View as Web Page** to turn on Web view.

④ To display the channel bar, check the **Internet Explorer Channel Bar** check box.

⑤ Click the **OK** button.

⑥ The desktop is displayed as a Web page.

Task 11: Working with Channels

Channels are sites designed specifically for Internet Explorer. You can have content from any of these channels delivered right to your desktop. (For more information about browsing the Internet and channels, see Part 9.)

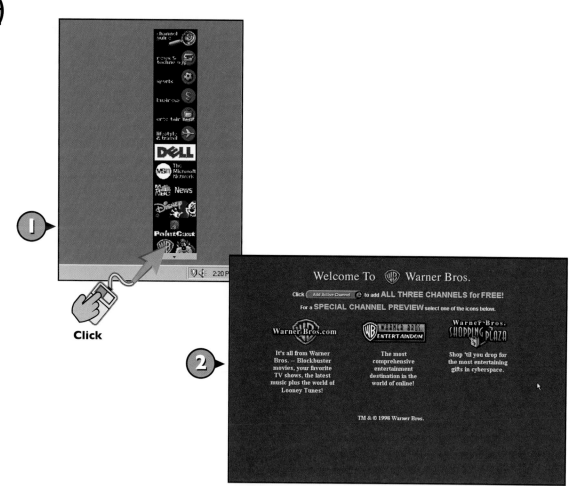

Start Here

Click

Welcome To Warner Bros.

Click **Add Active Channel** to add **ALL THREE CHANNELS for FREE!**

For a **SPECIAL CHANNEL PREVIEW** select one of the icons below.

Warner Bros.com — It's all from Warner Bros. -- Blockbuster movies, your favorite TV shows, the latest music plus the world of Looney Tunes!

WARNER BROS ENTERTAINDOM — The most comprehensive entertainment destination in the world of online!

Warner Bros. SHOPPING PLAZA — Shop 'til you drop for the most entertaining gifts in cyberspace.

TM & © 1998 Warner Bros.

✓ You can subscribe to certain channels and have the content downloaded according to the schedule you specify. You can also add other channels to your channel bar. For more information, consult online help or Part 9.

✓ To hide the channel bar, right-click a blank area of the desktop, choose **Active Desktop**, and click **View As Web Page** to deselect it.

1 ▶ To view a channel, click it.

✓ If you have not yet viewed the content, you will see a link. Click it to connect to your Internet provider and download the content.

2 ▶ Windows opens a full view of the channel window and displays the content if that content has been downloaded or viewed before.

End Task

Task 12: Changing the System Date and Time

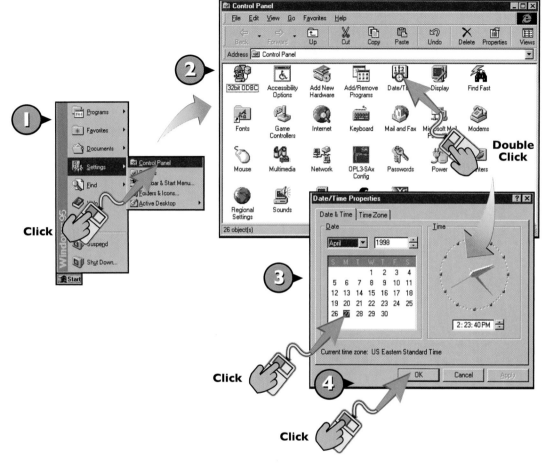

Windows displays the current time in the taskbar. You can place the pointer over the time to display the current date. If your system clock is wrong, you can correct it; you should do so because Windows places a time and date stamp on every file you save, identifying it for later use.

✓ If the date is wrong the next time you start your computer, it could indicate that you have a dead battery. If you need help replacing it, check your computer's documentation.

✓ Use the **Time Zone** tab to select the correct time zone for your area.

✓ To correct the date, click the correct date in the calendar. Use the drop-down list to select the correct month, and the spin box to select the correct year.

✓ You can use the up and down arrows to adjust the time.

① Click the **Start** menu, click **Settings**, and select **Control Panel**.

② Double-click the **Date/Time** icon.

③ Correct the date and time.

④ Click the **OK** button.

Task 13: Changing How the Mouse Works

You can adjust the mouse buttons and double-click speed to make using the mouse more comfortable for you. Suppose, for example, that you are left-handed; switching the left and right mouse buttons can make your work much easier. Likewise, if you are having trouble getting the double-click right, you can change the double-click speed on the mouse. You can also slow your pointer speed down so that you can easily find your mouse onscreen when you move it quickly.

Start Here

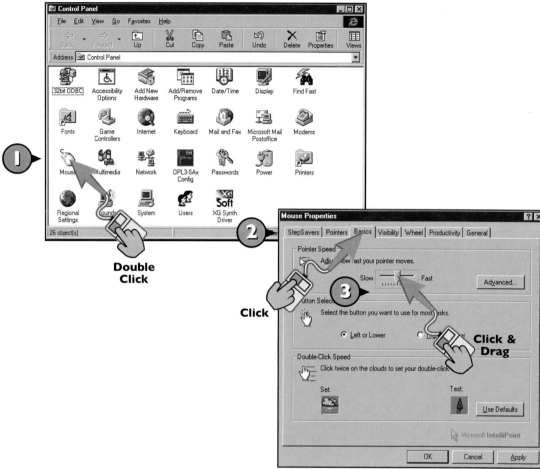

Double Click

Click

Click & Drag

✓ Depending on your mouse type, you may have additional tabs. For instance, if you have the Microsoft IntelliPoint mouse, you have tabs for StepSavers, Visibility, Productivity, Wheel, and so on. Click any of these tabs to make a change.

1 ▸ Double-click the **Mouse** icon in the **Control Panel** (refer to Task 12 if you need help opening the Control Panel).

2 ▸ If it is not already open, click the **Basics** tab.

3 ▸ Adjust the pointer speed by dragging the **Pointer speed** lever between **Slow** and **Fast**.

Next Step

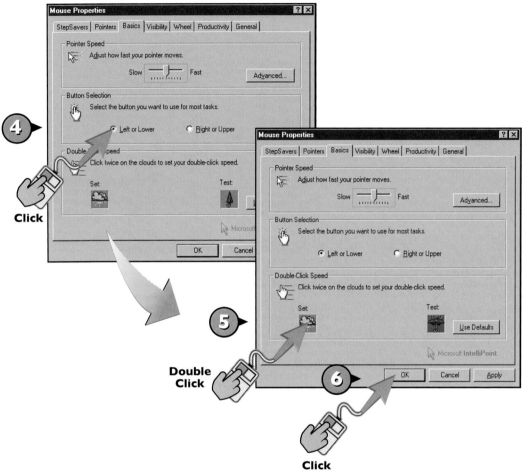

Click

Double Click

Click

(4) If you want to switch the mouse buttons, select the **Left or Lower** radio button.

(5) To change the double-click speed, click twice on the clouds to set your speed. You can test the speed by double-clicking the umbrella.

(6) Click the **OK** button.

✓ To go back to the default values for the mouse settings, click the **Use Defaults** button.

✓ The icon for setting the speed will vary. You may see a jack-in-the-box instead of a cloud and umbrella.

Task 14: Changing How the Mouse Pointers Look

You can easily change the way the mouse pointer appears onscreen. Depending on the action, the pointer takes several different shapes. For instance, when Windows is busy, you see an hourglass. You can select a different set of shapes (called a *scheme*) if you prefer.

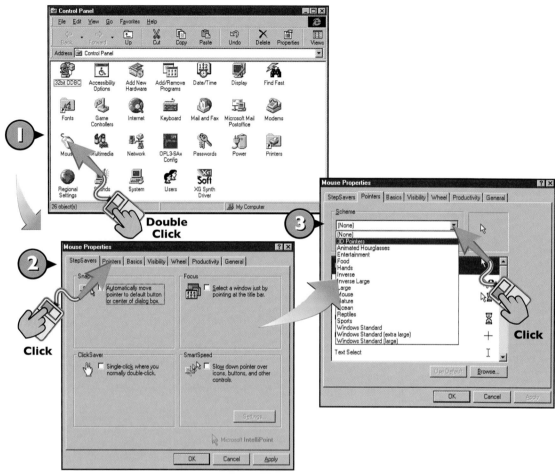

Click

Double Click

Click

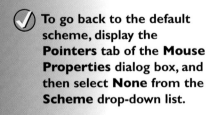
To go back to the default scheme, display the **Pointers** tab of the **Mouse Properties** dialog box, and then select **None** from the **Scheme** drop-down list.

1 ▶ Double-click the **Mouse** icon in the **Control Panel** (refer to Task 12 if you need help opening the Control Panel).

2 ▶ Click the **Pointers** tab.

3 ▶ Display the **Scheme** drop-down list and choose the scheme you want to use.

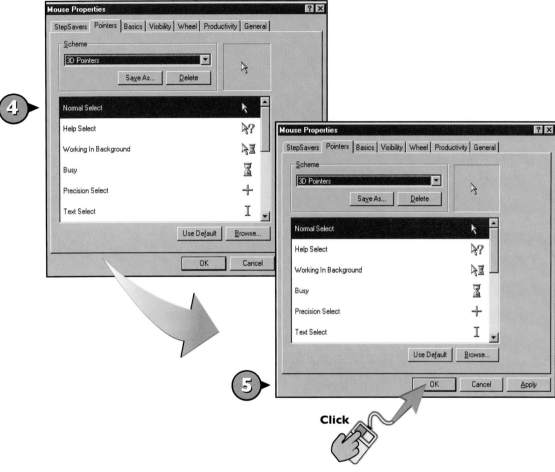

Click

4. A preview of each pointer in the chosen scheme (in this case, **3D Pointers**) is displayed.

5. Click **OK** to accept the changes and to close the dialog box.

✓ You can select which pointer to use for each individual pointer. Simply select the pointer you want to change, click the **Browse** button, select the pointer you want to use, and click **Open**. Do this for each pointer you want to change, and then click the **OK** button.

Task 15: Playing Sounds for Certain Windows Actions

When you perform certain actions in Windows 95, you might hear a sound. For instance, you hear a sound when Windows 95 is started. You might hear a sound when an alert box is displayed. You can stick with the default sounds, or you can select a different sound to use for each key Windows event.

Start Here

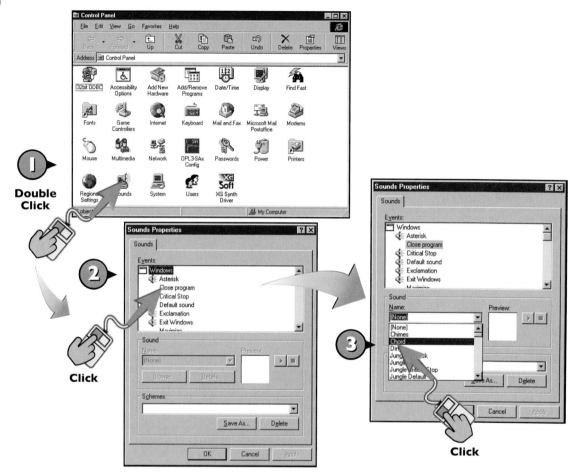

1 Double Click

2 Click

3

Click

✓ If you don't want a sound played for an event, select that event and choose **None** from the **Name** list.

✓ If you have sound schemes installed on your PC, you can select a set of sounds by displaying the **Schemes** drop-down list in the **Sound Properties** dialog box. Select the scheme you want and then click **OK**.

1 ▶ Double-click the **Sound** icon in the **Control Panel** (refer to Task 12 if you need help opening the **Control Panel**).

2 ▶ Select the sound event you want to change.

3 ▶ Display the **Name** drop-down list and select the sound that you want to assign.

Next Step

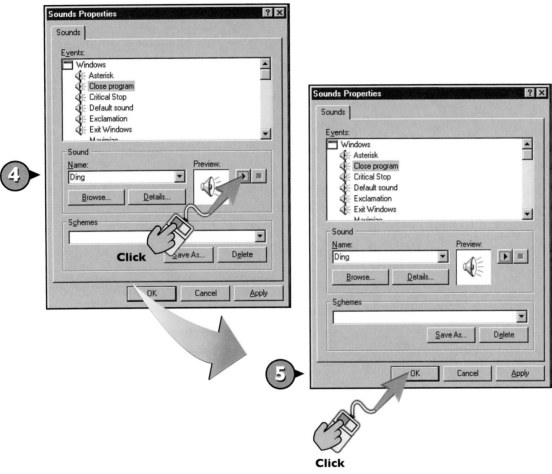

Click

Click

④ A preview icon becomes visible, and the **Play** button is activated. To hear a preview of the sound, click the **Play** button.

⑤ Click **OK** to accept the changes and to close the dialog box.

✓ **Events that have sounds associated with them are displayed with a speaker icon.**

If more than one person uses your PC, you might want to personalize certain Windows settings for each person. For instance, you can customize the desktop, **Start** menu, **Favorites** folder, Web page subscriptions, **My Documents** folder, and more. Each person can set up Windows the way he or she wants and then create a user profile. Each time that person logs on, all those settings will be used.

Task 16: Setting Up Windows for Multiple Users

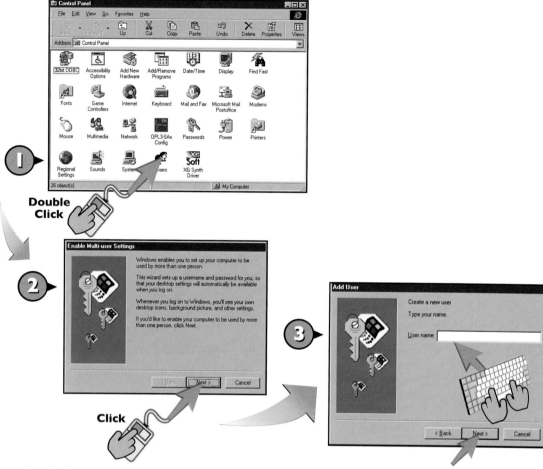

Double Click

Click

1 ▶ Double-click the **Users** icon in the **Control Panel** (refer to Task 12 if you need help opening the **Control Panel**).

2 ▶ Click the **Next** button.

3 ▶ Type the name of the person you are setting up, and then click **Next**.

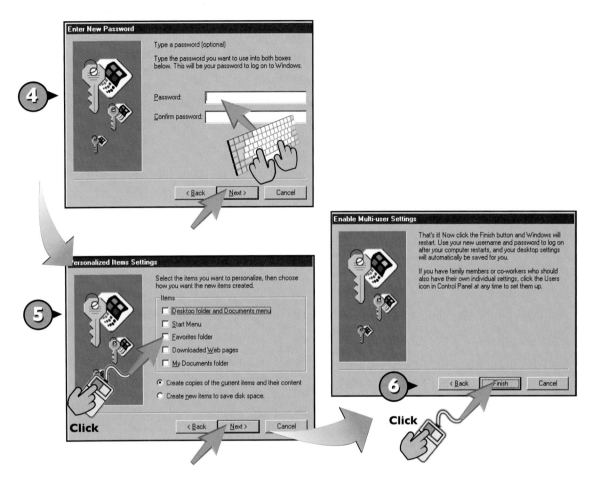

4 If you want to use a password to log on, type that password and then confirm the password by typing it again. After you finish, click **Next**.

5 From the **Items** section, select the items you want to save in this profile. After you finish, click **Next**.

6 Click the **Finish** button. Windows will be restarted, and you will be prompted to type your user name and password in order to log on.

 Follow this procedure to set up profiles for each user.

Task 17: Setting Up Windows for Special Needs

If you have special needs, you can turn on certain features of Windows 95 to make it easier to use. You can select different settings for the keyboard, sounds, display, and mouse.

Double Click

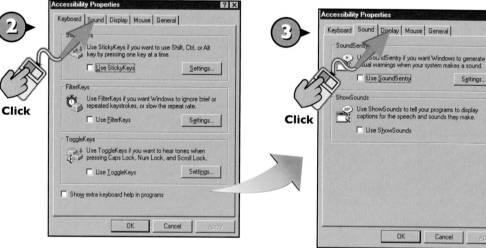

Click

Click

✓ Any changes you make in this dialog box can easily be reversed. Simply choose **Cancel** to close the dialog box.

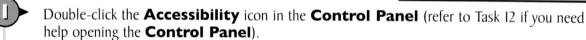

1 ▶ Double-click the **Accessibility** icon in the **Control Panel** (refer to Task 12 if you need help opening the **Control Panel**).

2 ▶ Enable any keyboard features by checking the appropriate check box. After you finish, click the **Sound** tab.

3 ▶ Select to display visual warnings and/or captions for alert messages, and then click the **Display** tab.

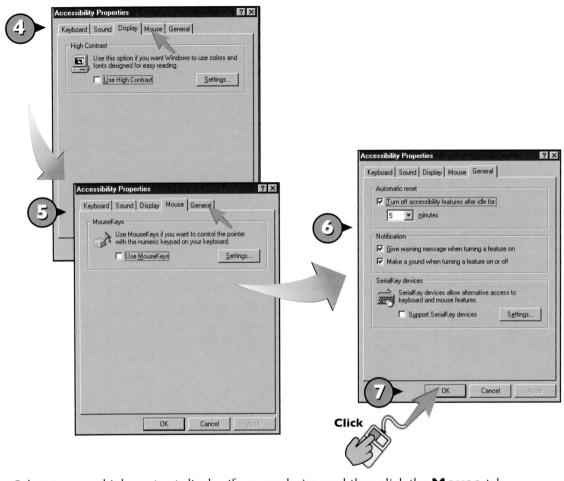

Click

4 Select to use a high-contrast display if you so desire, and then click the **Mouse** tab.

5 Select to use the numeric keypad to control the mouse, and then click the **General** tab.

6 Make changes as needed to the **Automatic reset** and **Notification** options.

7 Click the **OK** button.

You can use StickyKeys to press one key at a time for key combinations. Use FilterKeys to ignore brief repeated keystrokes. Use ToggleKeys to play a tone when you have pressed **Caps Lock, Num Lock,** or **Scroll Lock.**

End
Task

PART 6

Setting Up Programs

Most of the time you spend using your computer will be spent using some application. To make it as easy as possible, Windows 95 enables you to set up several ways for starting programs. You can create shortcuts to a program and place the shortcut on the desktop to make it more accessible. You can rearrange the programs on the **Start** menu so that they are more suited to how you work. You can install new programs and remove programs you no longer use. This part shows you how to accomplish all of these program setup tasks and more.

Tasks

Task 1: Adding Shortcuts

You can create shortcuts and place them on the desktop to provide quick access to programs. You then double-click a shortcut to quickly start that program—without having to open menus and folders.

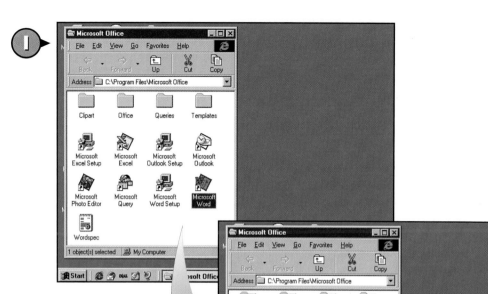

You can create shortcut icons to files or folders (covered in Part 3, "Working with Disks, Folders, and Files") or to your printer (covered in Part 4, "Printing with Windows").

1 In either **My Computer** or **Windows Explorer** (in this case, **My Computer**), display the program file for which you want to create a shortcut icon.

2 Holding down your right mouse button, drag the program file from the window to your desktop.

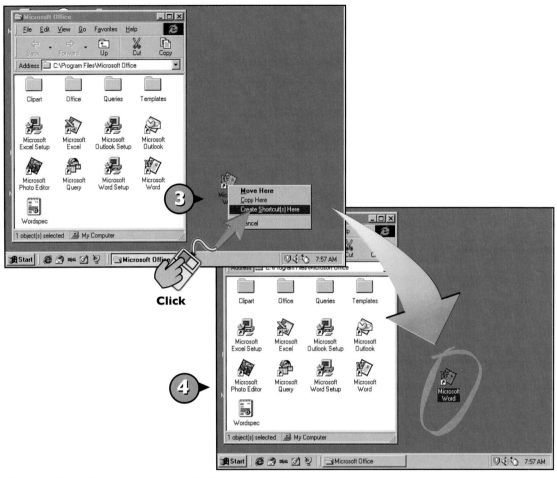

Click

3 ▶ Choose **Create Shortcut(s) Here** from the shortcut menu.

4 ▶ Windows adds the shortcut to your desktop.

✓ **If you can't find the program file, try searching for it. Finding a particular file is covered in Part 3.**

Task 2: Renaming Shortcuts

When you create a shortcut, Windows 95 assigns a name to the icon. However, you might want to use a different name. For instance, rather than the name **Word for Windows**, you might prefer just **Word**. You can rename any of the shortcut icons on your desktop.

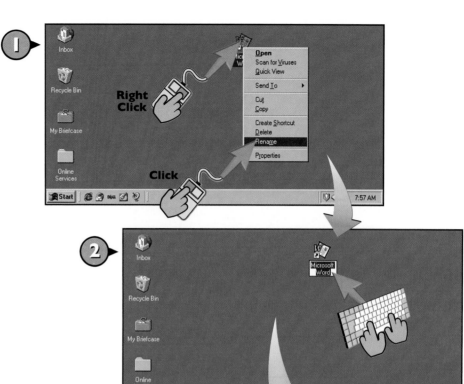

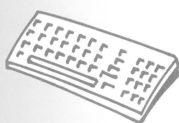

 Right-click the selected icon, and then click the **Rename** command.

Type the new shortcut name.

Press **Enter**, and the shortcut is renamed.

Task 3: Deleting Shortcuts

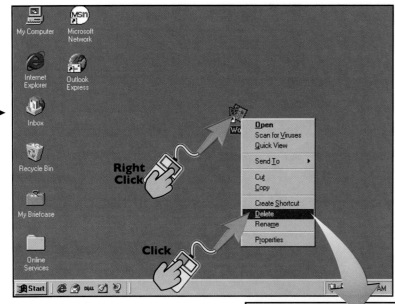

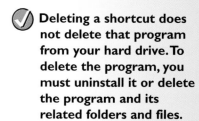

You can use shortcuts to quickly open the program you need. As time passes, however, your use for particular programs might change, and the desktop might become cluttered with program icons you no longer use. Just as you can create new shortcuts as you add new programs, you can delete shortcuts you no longer use.

✓ Deleting a shortcut does not delete that program from your hard drive. To delete the program, you must uninstall it or delete the program and its related folders and files.

✓ You can restore a shortcut from the **Recycle Bin**. To do so, double-click the **Recycle Bin** icon. In the **Recycle Bin** window, right-click the item you want to restore and choose **Restore**. The item returns to its original location. Close the **Recycle Bin** by clicking the **Close** (×) button.

1. Right-click the selected icon, and click the **Delete** command.

2. In the **Confirm File Delete** dialog box, click **Yes** to delete the shortcut.

Task 4: Adding Programs to the Start Menu

When you install most programs, they are added automatically to the **Start** menu. If a program is not added during installation, you can add it yourself.

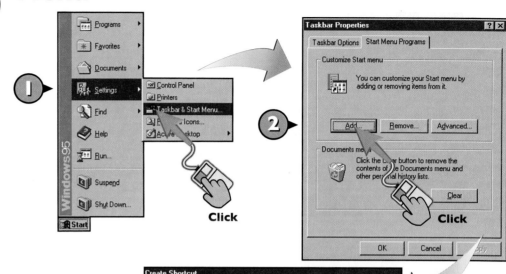

Click

Click

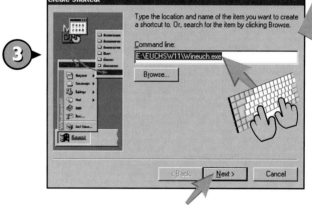

 To remove a program from the **Start** menu, see the next task.

 If you don't know the command line, click the **Browse** button, and then select the folder and the program name from the **Browse** dialog box.

1 Click **Start**, select the **Settings** command, and then click the **Taskbar & Start Menu** command.

2 Click the **Add** button in the **Start Menu Programs** tab (you might have to click this tab to view it).

3 Type the command line for the program you want to add and click the **Next** button.

Next Step

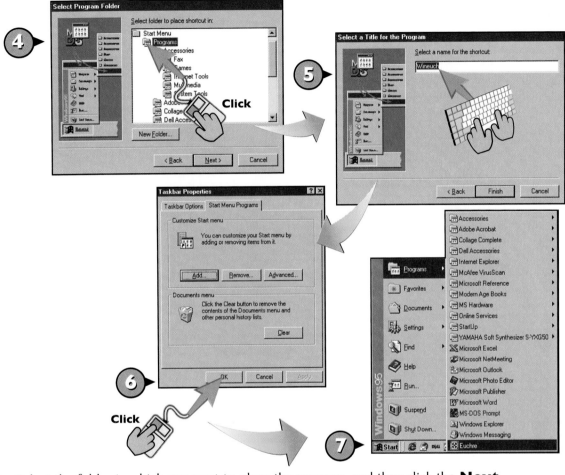

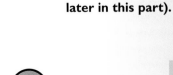

4 ▶ Select the folder in which you want to place the program, and then click the **Next** button.

5 ▶ Enter a name for the shortcut in the text box, or accept the one Windows displays. Click the **Finish** button.

6 ▶ Click the **OK** button to close the **Taskbar Properties** dialog box.

7 ▶ Display the **Start** menu to see the newly added program.

✓ **You can click the New Folder button to add a new folder (also see the task titled "Adding a Folder to the Start Menu" later in this part).**

End Task

Task 5: Deleting Programs from the Start Menu

At first, you might go a little crazy and add all kinds of icons. But after you use the computer more and more, you might want to streamline the **Start** menu and weed out programs that you don't use.

✓ You can follow this procedure to remove a folder from the **Start** menu. Simply select the folder and then click the **Remove** button. You are prompted to confirm the removal; click **Yes**. The folder and all its contents are removed.

✓ Keep in mind that removing a program from the **Start** menu does not remove the program and its files from your hard disk. To do this, you must uninstall the program or manually delete it and its related folders and files. See Task 10, "Uninstalling Applications," later in this part.

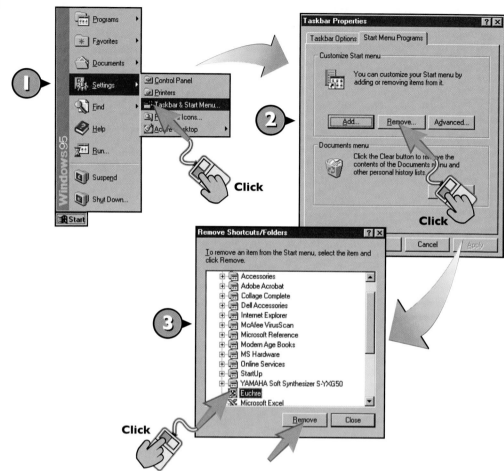

1 ▸ Click **Start**, select the **Settings** command, and then click the **Taskbar & Start Menu** command.

2 ▸ Click the **Remove** button in the **Start Menu Programs** tab. (you might have to click this tab to view it).

3 ▸ Select the program you want to remove and then click the **Remove** button.

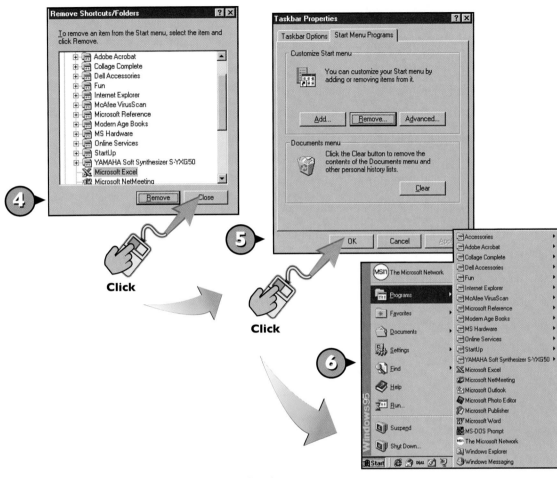

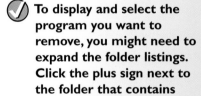

4 ▶ Click the **Close** button to close this dialog box.

5 ▶ Click **OK** to close the **Taskbar Properties** dialog box.

6 ▶ Display the **Start** menu and select **Programs** to verify that the program has been removed.

✓ **To display and select the program you want to remove, you might need to expand the folder listings. Click the plus sign next to the folder that contains the desired program.**

Task 6: Adding Folders to the Start Menu

When you install a new program, that program's installation sets up program folders and icons for itself. If you don't like the arrangement of the folders and icons, you can change it. For instance, if more than one person uses your PC, you might set up folders for each person and then add the programs that a certain person uses to his or her folder.

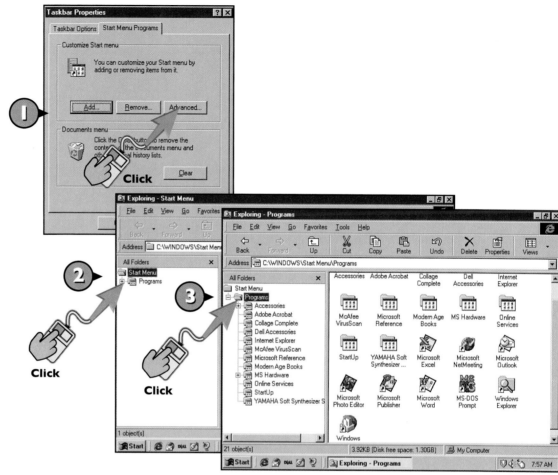

If you follow the steps in this task, you'll see the **Programs** folder in a **Windows Explorer** window. You can use any of the commands and features of Windows Explorer to work with the contents of your **Programs** folder.

 Click the **Advanced** button in the **Start Menu Programs** tab (refer to the last task if you need help displaying this tab).

 The **Start** menu is displayed in **Windows Explorer**. If needed, click the plus button next to the **Programs** entry to expand the list.

 Click the folder in which the new folder should be placed (in this example, I've clicked the **Programs** folder).

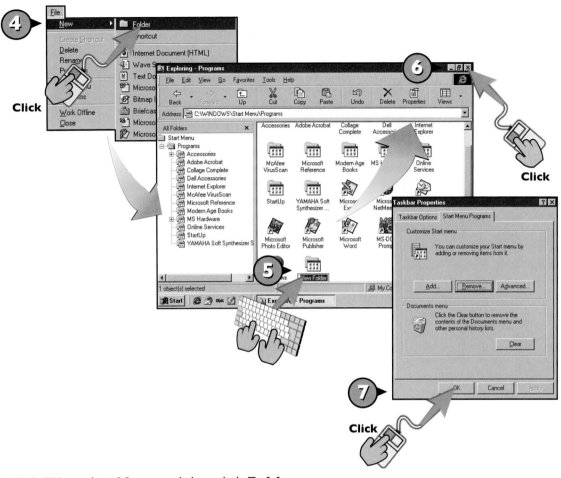

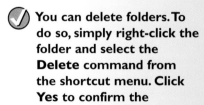

④ ► Click **File**, select **New**, and then click **Folder**.

⑤ ► Type the name for the new folder, and then press **Enter**.

⑥ ► Click the **Close** button.

⑦ ► Click the **OK** button in the **Taskbar Properties** dialog box.

✓ **You can delete folders. To do so, simply right-click the folder and select the Delete command from the shortcut menu. Click Yes to confirm the deletion.**

Task 7: Rearranging the Start Menu

After you set up folders, you can organize your **Start** menu, putting the program icons in the folder and order you want. For instance, you can create a **Fun** folder and put all your game programs in one folder.

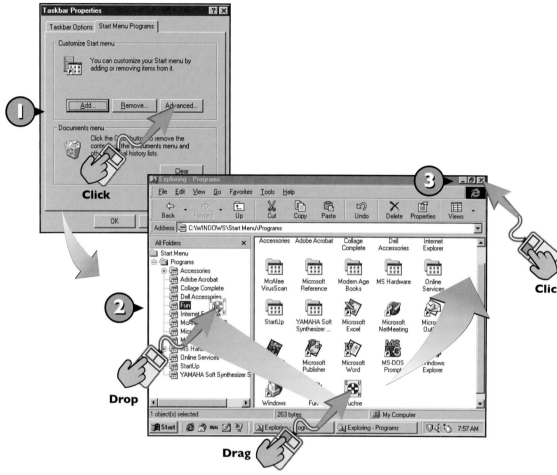

You can drag an existing program to a new location. Simply click the program name and then drag it to the new location on the **Start** menu.

1 ▶ Click the **Advanced** button in the **Start Menu Programs** tab (refer to Task 5 if you need help displaying this tab).

2 ▶ Click the desired icon or folder and then drag it to the folder where you want it placed. Do this for each program you want to move.

3 ▶ Click the **Close** button.

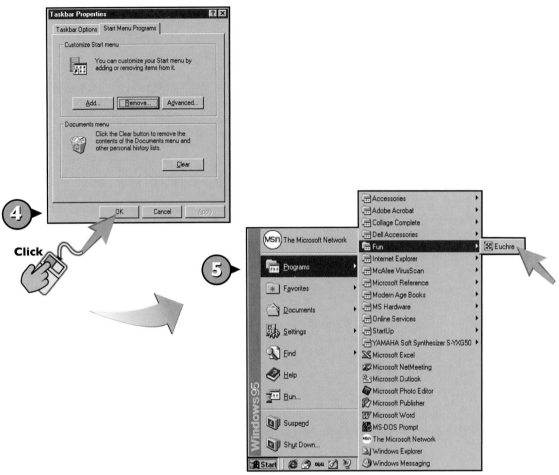

Click

4 ▶ Click the **OK** button in the **Taskbar Properties** dialog box.

5 ▶ Display the **Start** menu, click **Programs**, and then click **Fun** to verify that Euchre appears in the **Fun** folder.

Task 8: Starting an Application When You Start Windows

Windows enables you to start one or more programs at the same time that you start Windows. Each time you turn on your PC to start Windows, these applications will be opened as well. Applications you might want to open automatically include those that you use every day.

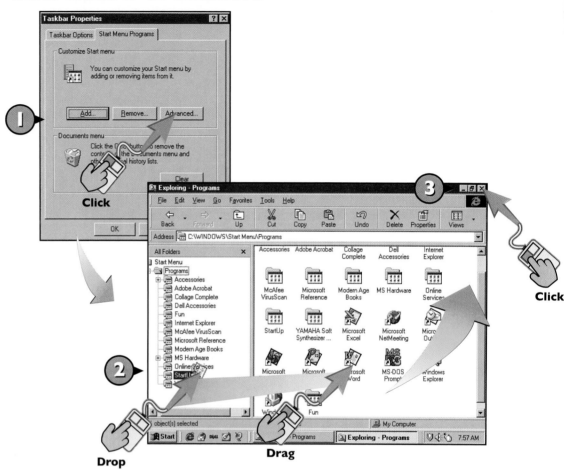

Click

Drop

Drag

Click

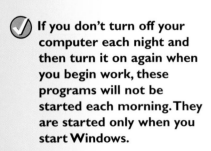

If you don't turn off your computer each night and then turn it on again when you begin work, these programs will not be started each morning. They are started only when you start Windows.

 Click the **Advanced** button in the **Start Menu Programs** tab (refer to Task 5 if you need help displaying this tab).

 Select the icon that represents the program that you want to add to your **Startup** folder (in this case, **Microsoft Word**). Hold down the **Ctrl** key and drag the icon to the **StartUp** folder.

 Click the **Close** button.

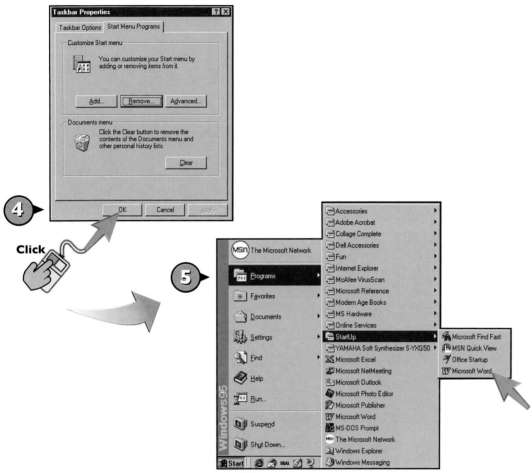

Click

4 Click the **OK** button in the **Taskbar Properties** dialog box.

5 Display the **Start** menu, click **Programs**, and then **StartUp** to verify that the **Microsoft Word** application appears in the **Startup** folder.

To remove an icon from the **StartUp** window, click the **Remove** button in the **Start Menu Programs** tab of the **Taskbar Properties** dialog box to display the **Remove Shortcuts/Folders** dialog box. Then choose the item you want to remove from the menu and click the **Remove** button. Close the **Remove Shortcuts/Folders** dialog box, and then click **OK**.

If necessary, expand the **Programs** list to display the **StartUp** folder.

Task 9: Installing Applications

When you bought your computer, it might have come with certain programs already installed. If you want to add to these, you can purchase additional programs and then add them to your system. Installing a new program basically copies the program files to a folder on your system and then adds a program icon for starting that program. The program's installation might also make changes to other files or programs on your system.

✓ If this procedure does not work, you can use the **Run** command to run the installation program. Insert the **CD-ROM** or disk into the appropriate drive, and then click the **Start** button and choose **Run**. Enter the disk drive and command for the installation program and click **OK**. Follow the onscreen instructions.

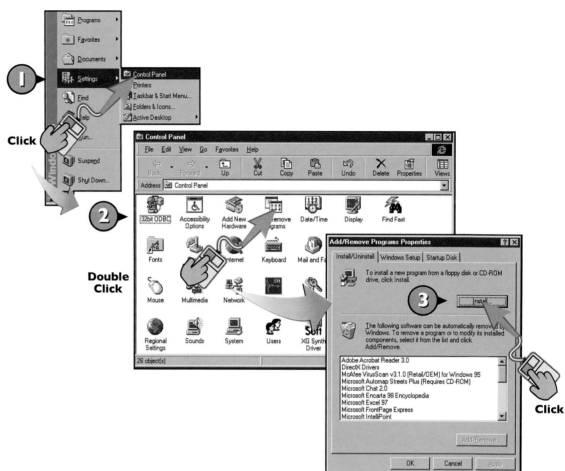

Click Start, select **Settings**, and click **Control Panel**.

Double-click the **Add/Remove Programs** icon.

Click the **Install** button in the **Install/Uninstall** tab.

Next Step

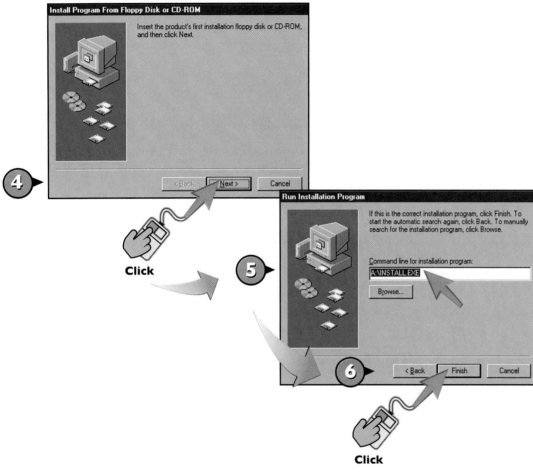

Click

Click

For help on uninstalling applications, see the next task.

The installation program usually adds an icon to your **Start** menu so that you can easily start the program. If it does not, you can add one for the program. Refer to Task 4, "Adding Programs to the Start Menu."

If the file isn't found automatically, click the **Browse** button and then open the drive and folder that contains the installation file. Select this file and click **OK**.

4 ▶ Insert the CD-ROM or floppy disk, and then click the **Next** button.

5 ▶ Windows looks for an installation program. When it finds this file, it displays it in the **Run Installation Program** dialog box.

6 ▶ Click the **Finish** button, and then follow the onscreen instructions for your particular program.

End Task

Task 10: Uninstalling Applications

You can easily remove a shortcut icon or an item from the **Start** menu, but doing so leaves that program on your hard disk. When you want to get rid of the program and its files entirely, you can uninstall it. Uninstalling a program removes the program and all its related files and folders from your hard disk.

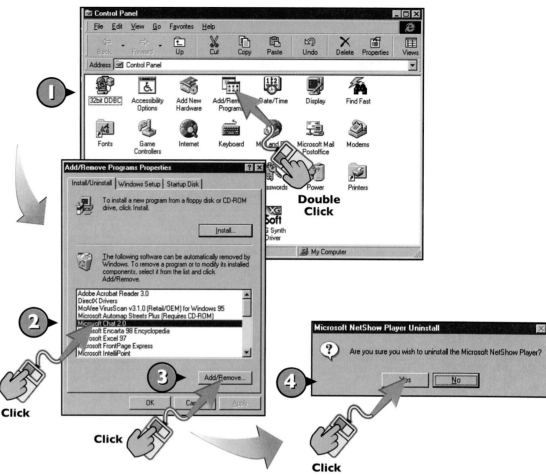

If your program is not listed in the **Install/Uninstall** tab, you must use a different procedure to uninstall it. Check your program documentation for specific instructions.

Depending on which application you are removing, the confirmation dialog might say **OK** instead of Yes.

1. Double-click the **Add/Remove Programs** icon in the **Control Panel** window (if you need help reaching this window, refer to the last task).

2. Click the program you want to remove.

3. Click the **Add/Remove** button.

4. If prompted to confirm the removal, click the **Yes** button. The program is removed from your system.

Task 11: Using the MS-DOS Prompt

Start Here

Sometimes you'll want to access the **DOS** prompt from Windows. For example, you might want to run a **DOS** application or use **DOS** commands. Alternatively, you might have programs (especially games) that run in **DOS**. You can run any program by typing the appropriate **DOS** command from the **MS-DOS** prompt.

✅ Your mouse will work in the **DOS Prompt** window only if you have loaded a mouse driver to **DOS**.

✅ You can use the icons at the top of the **DOS** window to mark, copy, and paste text; to enlarge the window to full screen; to set the background of the window; and to set the font.

✅ When you are finished working in **DOS**, click the **Close** button or type **exit** and press **Enter** to close the **MS-DOS Prompt** window.

① Click **Start**, select **Programs**, and click **MS-DOS Prompt**.

② Type the desired command and press **Enter**.

③ You can see the results of the command you typed.

End Task

Task 12: Installing Windows Components

If you have a new PC, it probably came with Windows already installed. As a result, you might not know which components are installed and which are not. If you want to add other components or simply to view what else might be available, you can do so.

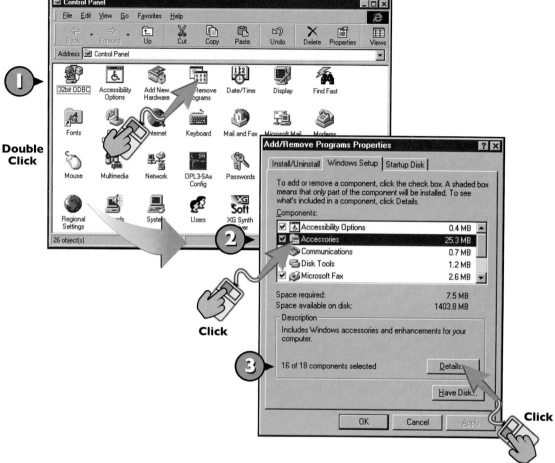

Double Click

Click

Click

If an item is checked, it is installed. Items that are gray and checked have some of the items installed.

1. Double-click the **Add/Remove Programs** icon in the **Control Panel** window (for help reaching this window, refer to Task 9).

2. In the **Windows Setup** tab, select the feature you want to change or check.

3. Click the **Details** button.

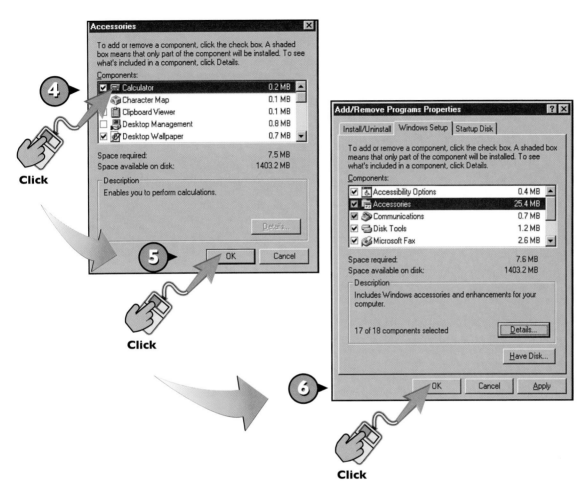

Click

Click

Click

④ ▶ You see a list of the available programs for this feature. Check the ones that you want to install, and uncheck any you want to uninstall.

⑤ ▶ Click the **OK** button.

⑥ ▶ After you insert your Windows CD-ROM, click the **OK** button in the **Add/Remove Programs Properties** dialog box. The necessary files are copied to your system.

You can also use the **Add/Remove Programs Properties** dialog box to create a startup disk. See Part 8 for information about creating this kind of disk.

End Task

PART 7

Using Windows Accessories

Windows 95 provides several accessories, or *applications*, that you can use to help you in your work. These accessories are not full-blown programs, but they are useful for specific jobs in the Windows environment. Accessories include a calculator, games, a painting program, a word processor, a text editor, and Internet applications. (The Internet applications and fax program are discussed in Part 9, "Getting Connected.") Windows 95 also includes some multimedia tools for playing CDs and for recording and playing back sounds. This part covers the basic applications included with Windows 95.

Tasks

Task 1: Playing Games

Start Here

Windows provides several games that you can play to break up your workday. Playing games is also a good way to help you get the hang of using the mouse. For instance, playing Solitaire can help you practice such mouse skills as clicking, dragging, and so on.

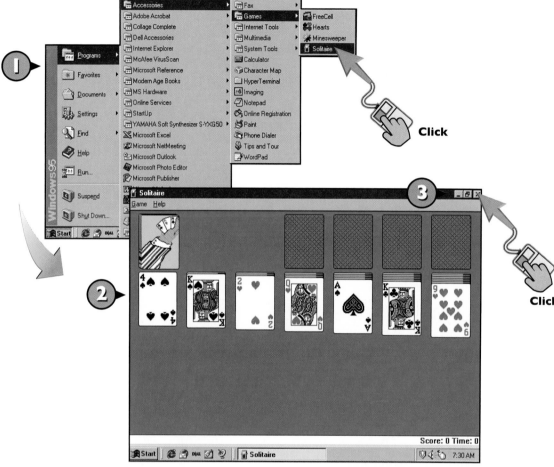

Click

Click

✓ If you don't see any games listed in your **Start** menu, they might not have been installed. You can easily add these Windows components to your system (refer to Task 12 "Installing Windows Components" in Part 6 of this book).

✓ If you aren't sure how to play a game, you can get instructions using the online help. Simply open the **Help** menu and then select **How To Play**.

 Click **Start**, select the **Programs** command, click the **Accessories** folder, click **Games**, and then click the name of the game you want to open (in this case, **Solitaire**).

 Play the game.

 When you are finished, click the **Close** button to exit.

End Task

Task 2: Starting WordPad

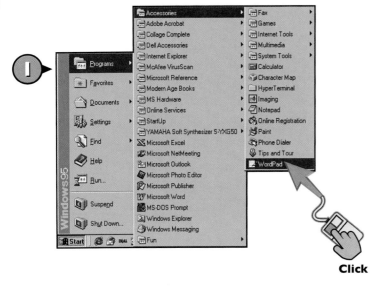

Click

Use WordPad to edit text files, or to create simple documents such as notes, memos, fax sheets, and so on. WordPad saves files in Word 6 for Windows format by default, but you can choose to save in a text-only format.

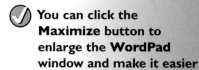

You can click the **Maximize** button to enlarge the **WordPad** window and make it easier to work in.

1. Click **Start**, select the **Programs** command, click the **Accessories** folder, and choose **WordPad**.

2. Use the menu bar to choose commands. Use the toolbar buttons as shortcuts for frequently used commands.

3. Use the format bar to make changes to the appearance of the text.

4. Use the ruler for setting tabs and indents.

To hide any of the screen elements in WordPad, open the **View** menu and click the tool you want to hide. A check mark indicates that the tool is showing; no check mark indicates that it is hidden.

Task 3: Typing Text

After you create a new document, you then type the text you want to include. The *insertion point* indicates where text will be entered as you type.

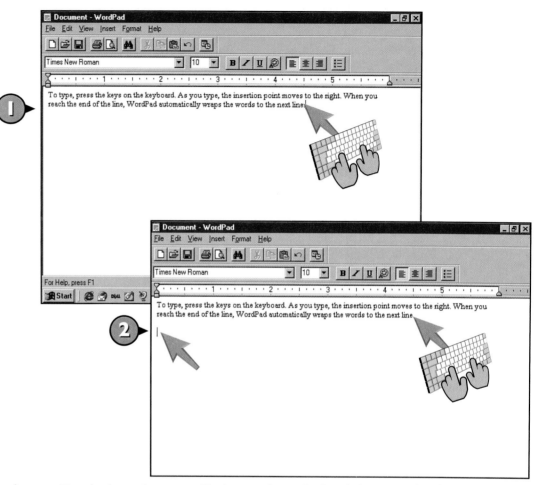

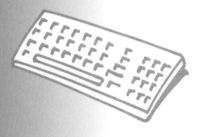

 If you make a mistake while typing, press the **Backspace** key to delete one character at a time. Then retype the text.

 Be sure to periodically save your document. For more information, refer to Task 8, "Saving a Document," in Part 2, "Using Applications in Windows 95."

Type the text. You don't need to press **Enter** at the end of each line; WordPad automatically wraps the lines within a paragraph.

To end a paragraph and start a new one, press **Enter**. The insertion point moves to the next line.

Task 4: Moving Around in a WordPad Document

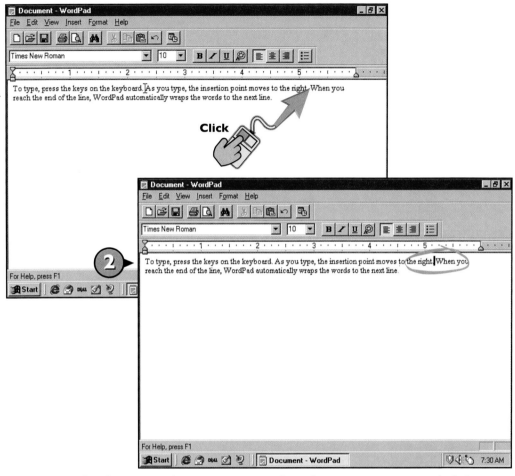

Click

To add new text or to select text for editing or formatting, you need to know how to move the insertion point to the spot where you want to make a change. You can use either the mouse or the keyboard to move the insertion point.

Point to the spot in the document where you want to place the insertion point, and click the mouse button.

The insertion point moves to that spot.

 Be sure to both point and click. If you simply point, the insertion point is not moved to the new location.

Task 5: Adding Text

One of the greatest things about using a word-processing program, even a simple one like WordPad, is how easily you can make changes. You can delete text, add text, and more. You can also polish the content of your document, making whatever changes are necessary.

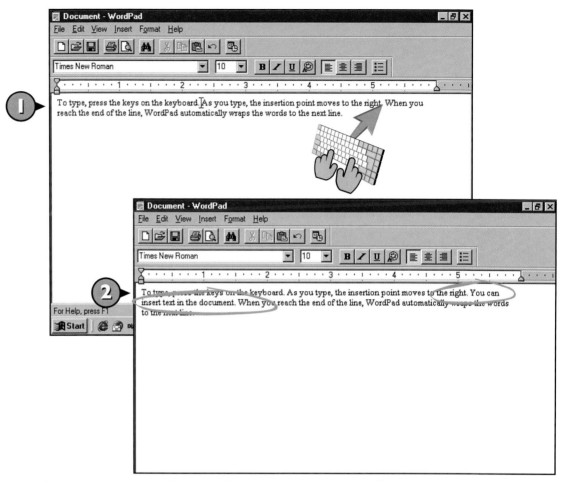

✓ If you make a mistake, you can undo the last action by clicking the **Edit** menu and choosing **Undo**.

✓ Be sure to save your document as you continue to work on it. Click **File** and then choose **Save** (or click the **Save** button on the toolbar). For more information, refer to Task 9, "Saving a Document," in Part 2.

✓ For information about copying or moving text, refer to Part 2.

 Move the insertion point to the spot where you want to make a change, and start typing.

 The existing text moves over to make room.

Task 6: Deleting Text

Start Here

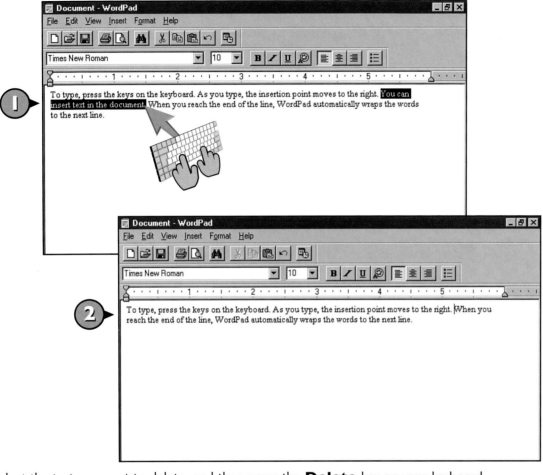

Just as you can add text, you can easily delete it. You can delete as little or as much text as needed—a character, a word, a sentence, a paragraph, or more. WordPad adjusts the existing text to fill the gap left by the text you delete.

1 Select the text you want to delete, and then press the **Delete** key on your keyboard.

2 The text is deleted.

✓ If you're not sure how to select text, refer to Task 11, "Selecting Text," in Part 2.

✓ If you make a mistake, you can undo the deletion by clicking the **Edit** menu and choosing **Undo**.

End Task

Task 7: Formatting Text

You can easily make simple changes to the appearance of text. For example, you can change the font or font size, and you can make text bold, italic, or underlined. This task touches on just a few of the formatting changes you can make. Experiment to try out some of the other available formatting features.

✓ You can use toolbar buttons to change many paragraph features. For example, use the **Alignment** buttons to change the alignment of the paragraph. Add bullets by clicking the **Bullets** button. You can also use the commands in the **Format** menu to change the appearance of your document.

✓ Save your document by clicking the **Save** button or by clicking **File** and then choosing **Save**. For more information on saving a document, refer to Part 2.

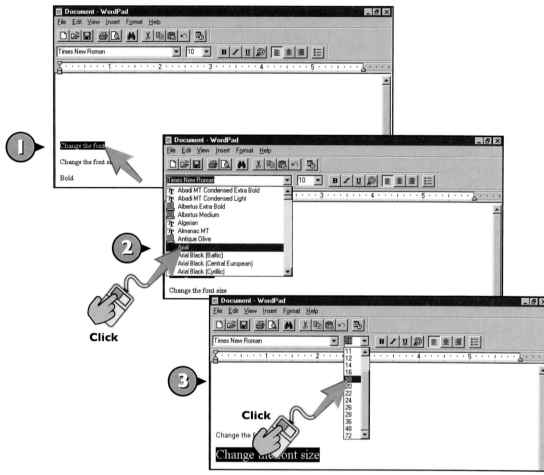

Click

Click

1 ▶ Select the text you want to change. If you need help selecting text, refer to Task 11 in Part 2.

2 ▶ To change the font, click the **Font** drop-down arrow and click the font you want.

3 ▶ To change the font size, select the text you want to change, click the **Font Size** drop-down arrow, and click the size you want to use.

 To make text bold, italic, or underlined, select the text you want to change, and then click the appropriate button in the format bar.

 To change the font color, select the text you want to change, click the **Font Color** button, and then click the color you want.

 To undo a change, click the Undo button in the toolbar.

Task 8: Using Notepad

The most common type of simple file is a *text file*. You can find instructions on how to install a program and other information in text files. Some configuration files are also text files. To edit and work with this type of file, you can use Notepad, a simple text editor provided with Windows 95.

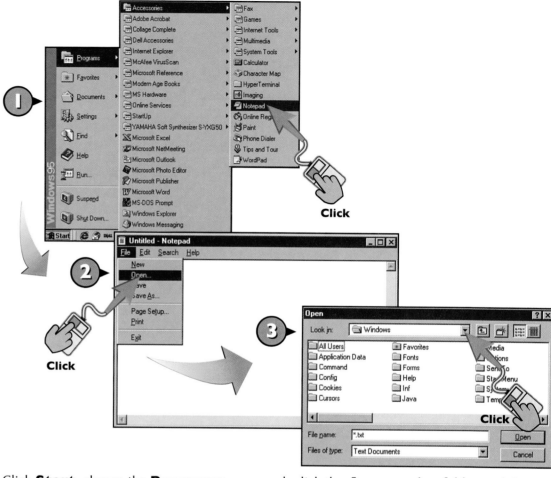

Click

Click

Click

✓ Be careful when making changes to any configuration text file. Be sure you know exactly what you are doing.

✓ By default, Notepad displays all text files. You can display all files by displaying the **Files of type** drop-down list and selecting **All Files (*.*)**.

1 ▶ Click **Start**, choose the **Programs** command, click the **Accessories** folder, and then choose **Notepad**.

2 ▶ To open a file in Notepad, click **File** and then choose **Open**.

3 ▶ Find the folder that contains your file. You can use the **Look in** drop-down list box to change to a different drive.

Next Step

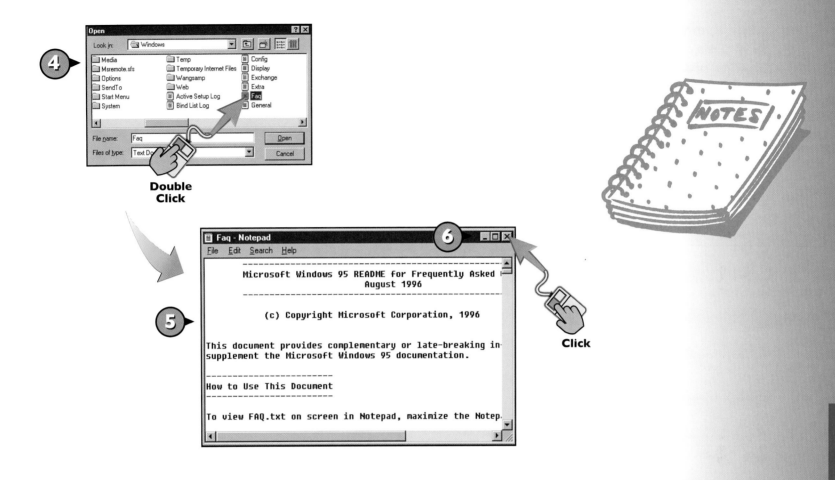

**Double
Click**

Click

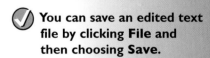

④ Double click the desired file to open it (in this case, **Faq**).

⑤ Review the file. If you want, you can also make any changes to the file.

⑥ To exit Notepad, click the **Close** button.

✓ You can save an edited text
file by clicking **File** and
then choosing **Save**.

Task 9: Using Paint

Use Paint to create art and to edit graphics such as clip art, scanned art, and art files from other programs. You can add lines, shapes, and colors, as well as alter the original components.

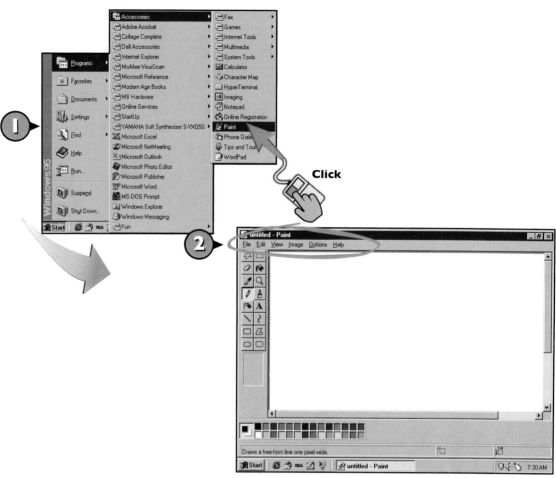

Click

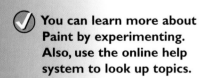 You can learn more about Paint by experimenting. Also, use the online help system to look up topics.

 Click **Start**, choose the **Programs** command, click the **Accessories** folder, and choose **Paint**.

 Use the menu bar to choose commands.

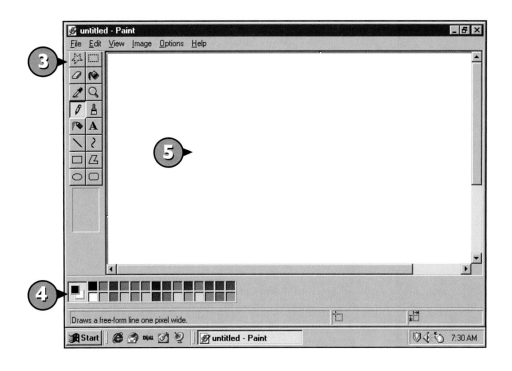

3 Use the toolbox to select the drawing tool you want to work with.

4 Use the color box to select colors for the lines and fills of the objects you draw.

5 Draw in the drawing area.

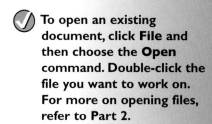 To open an existing document, click **File** and then choose the **Open** command. Double-click the file you want to work on. For more on opening files, refer to **Part 2**.

Task 10: Drawing a Shape

Start Here!

You can create many different types of shapes, including lines, curves, rectangles, polygons, ovals, circles, and rounded rectangles.

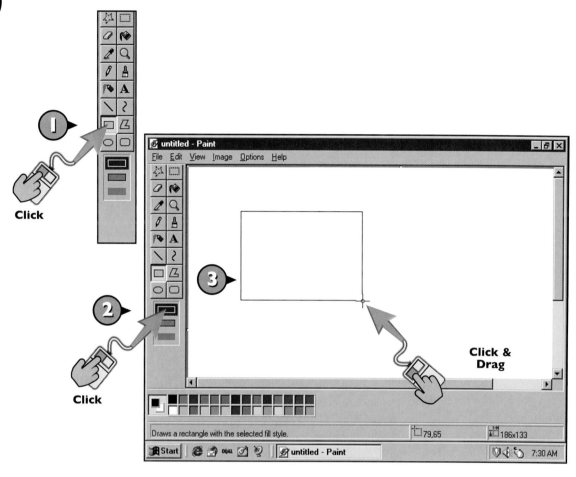

Click

Click

① Click the tool you want to draw with (in this case, the **Rectangle** tool).

② The toolbox displays options for the selected tool. In this case, choose whether you want to draw an empty rectangle, one that is filled and bordered, or one that is filled but not bordered.

③ Move the pointer into the drawing area. Click and drag to draw.

 Click the color bar at the bottom of the **Paint** window to choose a color. Click the color you want to use for the lines and borders. To select a fill color, right-click the color you want to use.

 If you do not like what you've drawn, open the **Edit** menu and choose **Undo** to undo the last action.

End Task

Task 11: Adding Text

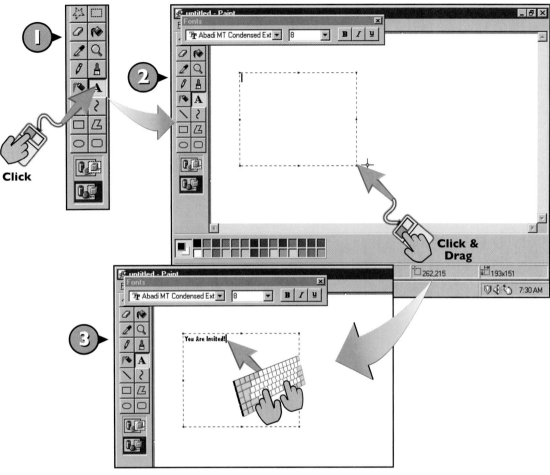

Click

Click & Drag

You can include text as part of your drawing. To do so, draw a text box and then type the text you want to include. You can include as much or as little text as you want. You can also change the appearance of the text.

✓ When you are typing the text, you see the **Fonts** toolbar. You can use the items in this toolbar to change the font and font size, and to make the text bold, italic, or underlined.

✓ You cannot edit the text once you've added it to the drawing. To change the text, you must delete the text box and start again.

①▶ Click the **Text** tool.

②▶ Move the pointer into the drawing area and drag to draw a text box.

③▶ Type the text you want to add. The text is added to the text box.

Task 12: Drawing Freehand

In addition to shapes and text, you can also draw freehand on the page. This is similar to drawing with a pencil or pen (only you are drawing in your document!).

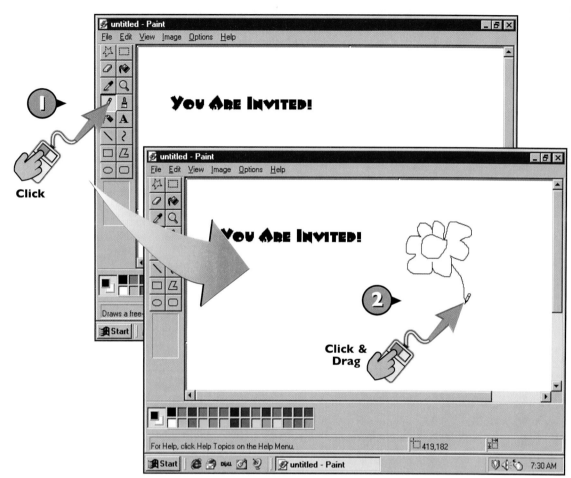

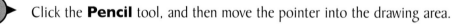

To erase your freehand marks, use the **Eraser** tool (see Task 13, "Erasing Part of a Drawing").

To draw in a different color, click the color you want to use in the color box before you drag to draw.

1 ▶ Click the **Pencil** tool, and then move the pointer into the drawing area.

2 ▶ Hold down the mouse button and drag the pencil icon to draw.

Task 13: Erasing Part of a Drawing

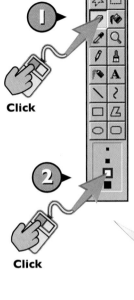

Click

Click

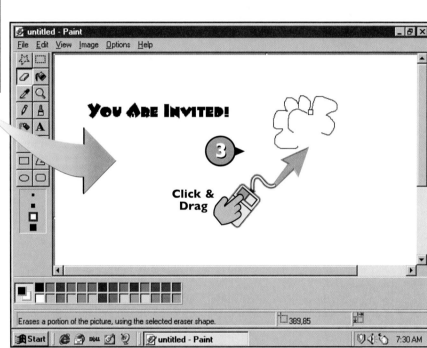

If you make a mistake and want to get rid of something you have added, you can use the **Eraser** tool. You can erase any part of the drawing.

✓ To erase a selected part of a drawing, click the **Select** tool and drag the mouse across part of your drawing. Press the **Delete** key to remove the selected part of the drawing.

✓ To clear everything on the page, click **Image**, and then choose **Clear Image**.

✓ You can select the size of the eraser you want to use. Click the **Eraser** tool, and then click the size you want to use in the toolbox.

① ▸ Click the **Eraser** tool.

② ▸ Select the size of the eraser.

③ ▸ Move the pointer to the drawing area. Hold down the mouse button and drag across the part you want to erase.

Task 14: Adding Color to a Drawing Using the Brush Tool

There are many ways to add color to a drawing. One way is to use the **Brush** tool. This is similar to "painting" onscreen with a paintbrush. You can select from several brush sizes and styles.

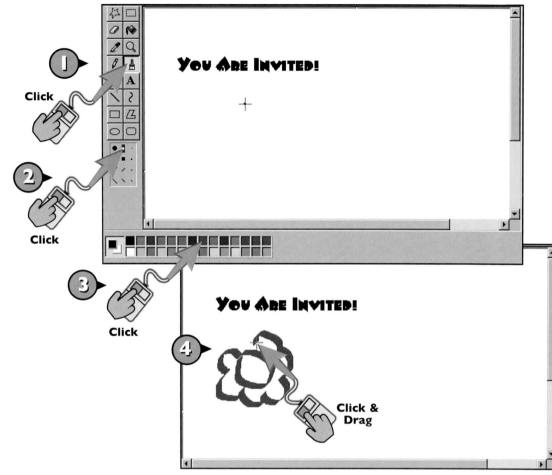

Start Here

Click

Click

YOU ARE INVITED!

Click

YOU ARE INVITED!

Click & Drag

You can also spray paint color on the page or fill an item with color. See the next two tasks.

 Click the **Brush** tool.

 Click the brush size and shape.

 Click the color you want to use in the color box.

 Hold down the mouse button and drag across the page to "paint" with the brush.

 End Task

Task 15: Adding Color to a Drawing Using the Airbrush Tool

Start Here

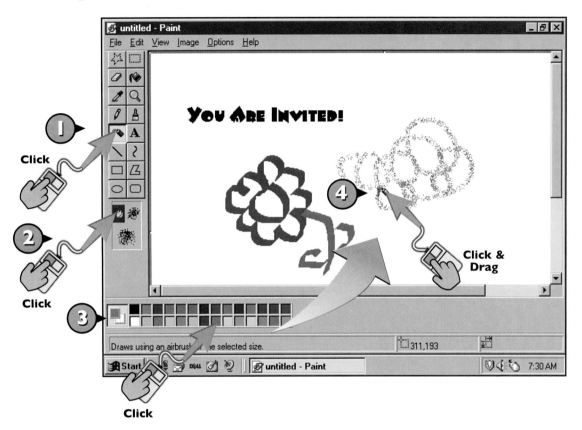

Click

Click

Click

Click & Drag

In addition to using a paint brush, you can "spray paint" color onto a page using the **Airbrush** tool. You can select different splatter sizes and also select the color to use.

 Click the **Airbrush** tool.

 Click the splatter size you want.

 Click the color you want to use.

 Hold down the mouse button and drag across the page to "spray paint" that color on the page.

 The splatter size controls the density of the spray-paint pattern. You can select from three different splatter sizes.

End Task

Task 16: Adding Color to a Drawing Using the Fill with Color Tool

You can use the **Fill with Color** tool to fill an object or drawing area with color. For instance, you can fill a rectangle or circle with any of the colors available in the color palette.

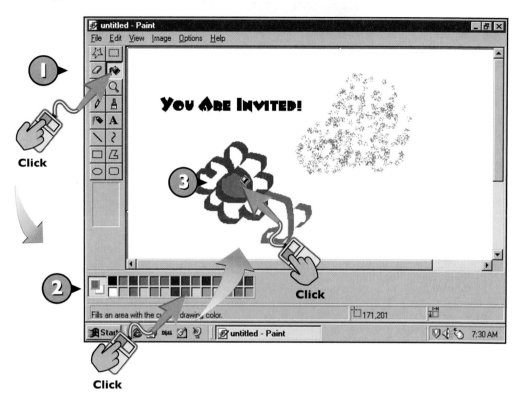

If color spills outside the area you intended to fill, that probably means you tried to fill an area that was not closed. Be sure that you are filling an area that is bordered on all sides.

1 Click the **Fill with Color** tool.

2 Click the color you want to use.

3 Click inside the area you want to paint. That area is filled with color.

Task 17: Using Calculator

Start Here

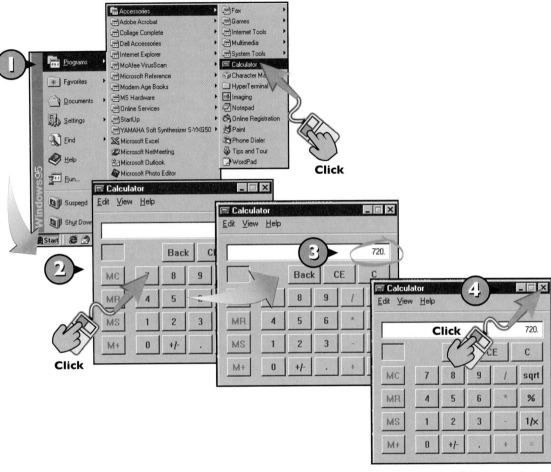

Click

Click

Click

If you need to perform a quick calculation, use the Calculator program included with Windows 95. You can use this handy tool to add, subtract, multiply, divide, figure percentages, and more.

✓ To use a more complex scientific calculator, click the calculator's **View** menu and then click **Scientific**.

✓ You can copy the results of a calculation into a document. To do so, select the results, click **Edit**, and then choose **Copy**. Then move to the document where you want to paste the results, click **Edit**, and then choose **Paste**.

✓ To use the numeric keypad to enter numbers, press the **Num Lock** button. Then type the equation using these keys.

1 ▶ Click **Start**, choose the **Programs** command, choose the **Accessories** folder, and then click **Calculator**.

2 ▶ Click the buttons on the calculator to enter an equation.

3 ▶ You see the results of the calculation.

4 ▶ When you are finished, click the **Close** button.

End Task

Task 18: Playing a Sound with Sound Recorder

You can use various Windows multimedia devices, such as the Sound Recorder, to add to the presentations or documents you create in Windows. Use Sound Recorder to record your own sounds and insert the sound files into your documents for clarification or interest. To use the multimedia features of Windows 95, you need a sound card and speakers.

✓ You can record sounds using Sound Recorder. To do so, you must have an audio input device (microphone) attached to your PC. Click **File**, choose **New**, and then click the **Record** button and record your sound. To stop recording, click the **Stop** button. To save your sound, click **File** and then choose **Save As**.

✓ If you cannot hear the sound, adjust the volume on your speakers.

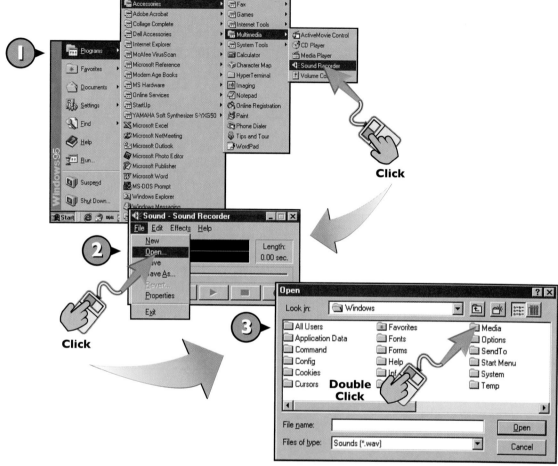

Click

Click

Double Click

1 ▸ Click **Start**, choose the **Programs** command, choose the **Accessories** folder, click the **Multimedia** folder, and choose **Sound Recorder**.

2 ▸ Click the **File** menu, and then choose **Open**.

3 ▸ Double-click the folder that contains the sound file. (To sample one of Windows' sounds, select the **Windows\Media** folder.)

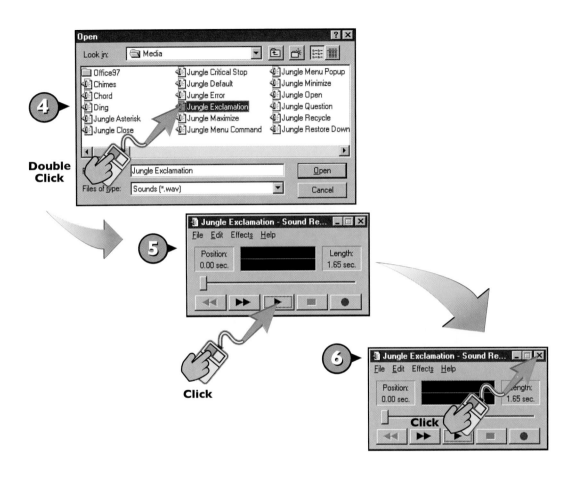

Double Click

Click

④ Double-click the sound file you want to play.

⑤ Click the **Play** button.

⑥ Click the **Close** button to close the **Sound Recorder** window.

Task 19: Playing an Audio CD

In addition to being able to play back sound files, you can play audio CDs using **CD Player**, enabling you to listen to the background music of your choice as you work. Note that in order to use the multimedia features of Windows 95, you need a sound card and speakers.

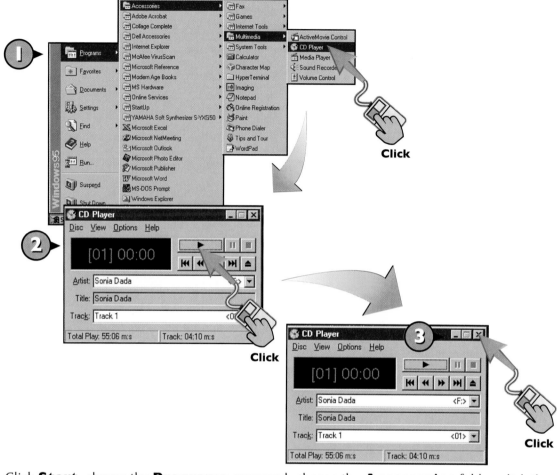

Click

Click

Click

 If you insert a CD, CD Player will start automatically.

 To stop playing, click the **Stop** button. To close the **CD Player** window and exit CD Player, click the **Close** button.

 To play a different track, display the **Track** dropdown list and select the track you want to play.

Click **Start**, choose the **Programs** command, choose the **Accessories** folder, click the **Multimedia** folder, and choose **CD Player**.

After you insert your CD into your CD drive, click the **Play** button in the **CD Player** window.

When you're finished, click the **Close** button to close the **CD Player** window.

Task 20: Changing the Volume

Start Here

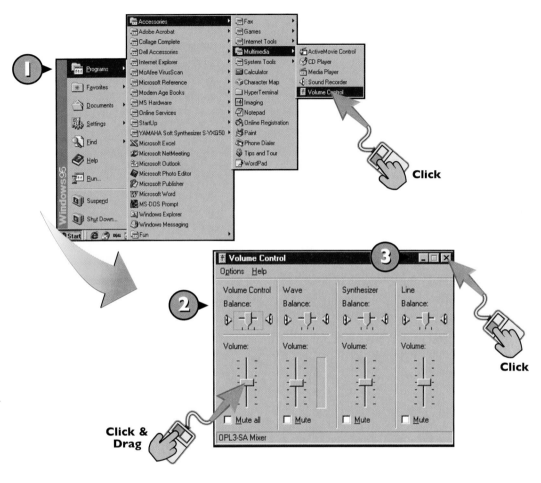

Click

Click

Click & Drag

To adjust the volume of your multimedia programs, use **Volume Control.** You can set the volume and balance for different types of sounds.

① Click **Start**, choose the **Programs** command, choose the **Accessories** folder, click the **Multimedia** folder, and choose **Volume Control**.

② Drag any of the volume control bars in the **Volume Control** window to adjust the volume.

③ Click the **Close** button to close Volume Control.

✓ You might also have a volume control on your speakers. You can use these to also adjust the sound.

✓ To display the **Volume Control** panel, you can double-click the **Speaker** icon in the taskbar.

End Task

Task 21: Playing a Media File

Media files are a combination of text, graphics, sounds, video, and animations. As computers take more and more advantage of the multimedia features of your PC, you will find more media files for your use. For instance, Windows 95 comes with some sample media files. To play these presentations, you can use Media Player.

Start Here

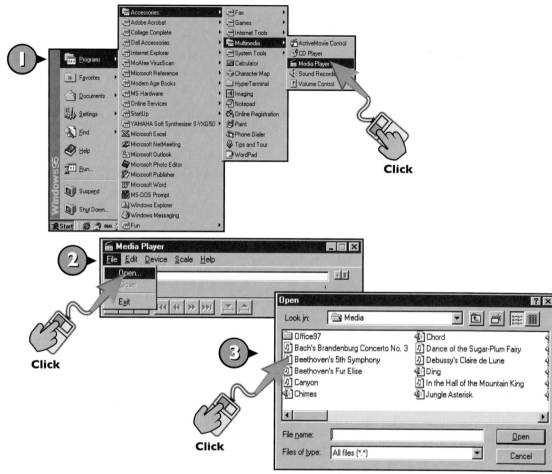

Click

Click

Click

✓ If you have no media files available, it might be because these files were not installed when Windows was set up. You can add other components, including sample media files. See Task 12, "Installing Windows Components," in Part 6, "Setting Up Programs."

1 ► Click **Start**, choose the **Programs** command, choose the **Accessories** folder, click the **Multimedia** folder, and choose **Media Player**.

2 ► In the **Media Player** window, click **File** and then choose **Open**.

3 ► Navigate to the folder that contains the media file you want to play, and then double-click that file.

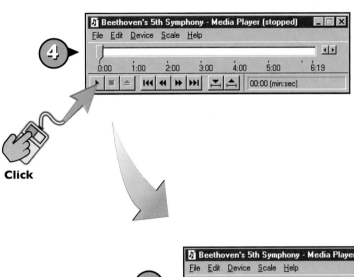

4 Click the **Play** button.

5 The media file is played. To close Media Player, click the **Close** button.

✓ The Internet includes many types of media files. For information on browsing the Internet, see Part 9, "Connecting to Online Services and the Internet."

✓ To sample the media files provided by Windows 95, navigate to the Windows/Media folder.

Maintaining Your System

This part of the book introduces some techniques that are useful for maintaining your system: defragmenting a disk, backing up data files, scanning a disk for damage, and others.

To safeguard your data files, you should periodically make an extra copy, called a *backup*. You can use the backup program included with Windows 95 to make backing up easy. You should also perform other periodic system maintenance, as covered here.

Tasks

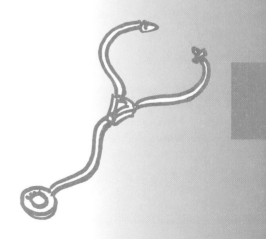

Task 1: Displaying Disk Information

You can display information about your disks, such as the size, the amount of space taken, and the amount of free space. You can also enter a label for a disk; this label is used in file windows to identify the disk.

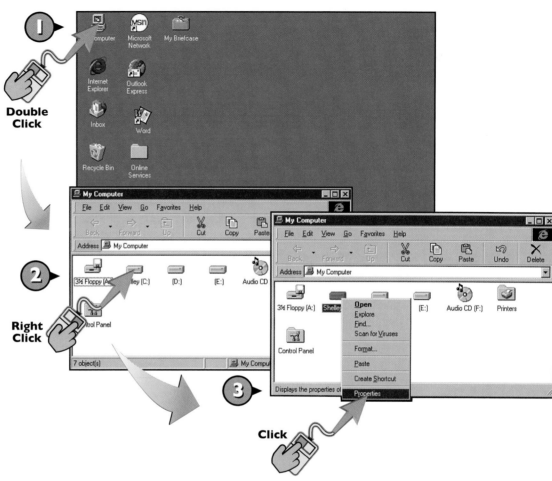

Double Click

Right Click

Click

✓ If you are working in Web view, you can single-click My Computer to display its contents.

1 ► Double-click the **My Computer** icon.

2 ► In the **My Computer** window, right-click the disk for which you want information.

3 ► Click **Properties**.

Next Step

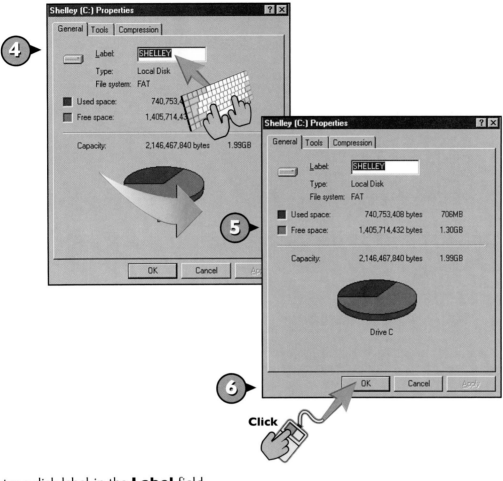

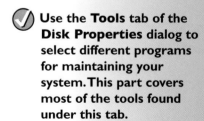

4 Enter a disk label in the **Label** field.

5 View information about used and free space.

6 Click the **OK** button to close the dialog box.

Click

✓ Use the **Tools** tab of the **Disk Properties** dialog to select different programs for maintaining your system. This part covers most of the tools found under this tab.

End
Task

Task 2: Scanning Your Disk for Errors

Sometimes parts of your hard disk get damaged. You might see an error message when you try to open or save a file, or you might notice lost or disarrayed data in some of your files. You can scan the disk for damage using the ScanDisk program and fix any problems. You must also run ScanDisk before you can defragment a hard disk (covered next).

✔ If you don't properly shut down Windows, you are prompted to run ScanDisk when you reboot. You can then check for errors before your system is restarted.

✔ If **ScanDisk** is not listed on the **System Tools** menu, it could indicate that this program was not installed when you installed Windows. Refer to Task 12, "Installing Windows Components," in Part 6, "Setting Up Programs."

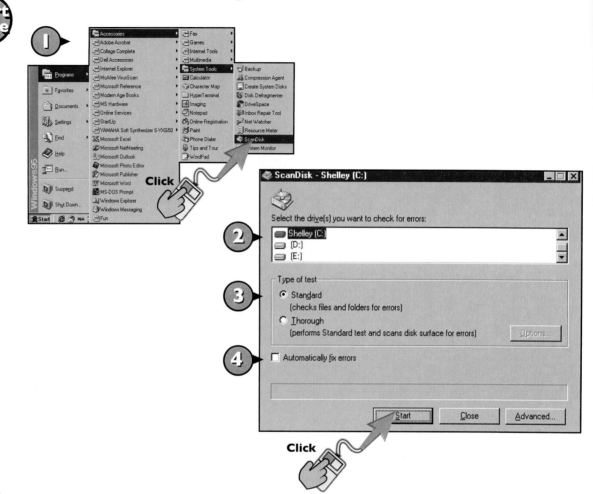

1 ▶ Click **Start**, choose the **Programs** command, select the **Accessories** folder, click the **System Tools** folder, and choose **ScanDisk**.

2 ▶ Select the drive you want to scan.

3 ▶ Click the radio button next to the type of test you want (**Standard** or **Thorough**).

4 ▶ Specify whether you want ScanDisk to automatically fix errors by checking or unchecking the **Automatically fix errors** check box, and then click the **Start** button.

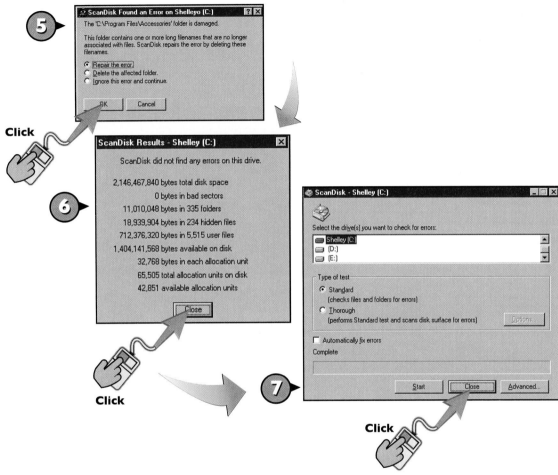

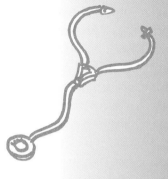

Click

Click

Click

5 ⟩ If ScanDisk finds an error, a dialog box appears to explain it. Read the error message, and choose the option that best suits your needs. Click **OK** to continue. Do this for each message.

6 ⟩ When ScanDisk finishes, it displays a report of the scan. Click **Close** to return to the **ScanDisk** dialog box.

7 ⟩ Click the **Close** button to exit ScanDisk.

✓ **The main difference between the standard and thorough tests is that the thorough test methodically checks each sector of the disk in detail, and takes up to four times as long to complete than the standard. Try the standard test first; if it finds problems it cannot fix, then perform the thorough test.**

Task 3: Defragmenting a Disk

When a file is stored on your hard drive, Windows places as much of the file as possible in the first available section (called a *cluster*) and then goes to the next cluster to place the next part of the file. Initially, this storage does not cause performance problems, but over time, your disk files become *fragmented*; you might find that it takes a long time to open a file or start a program. To speed access to files and to help prevent potential problems with fragmented files, you can defragment your disk, putting files in clusters as close to each other as possible. Defragmenting your disk is a general-maintenance job that you should perform every few months for best results.

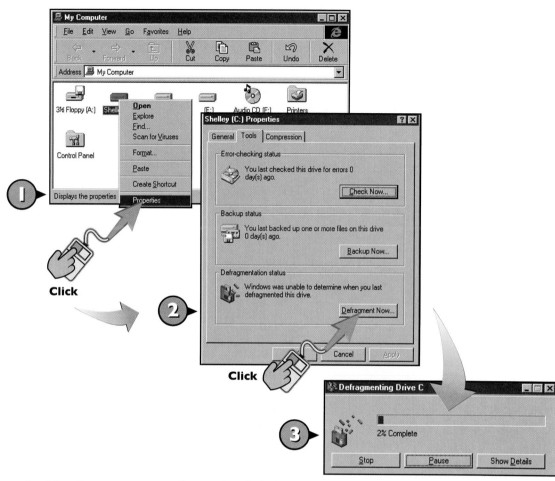

1 In the **My Computer** window, right-click the disk you want to defragment and choose **Properties** (if you need help reaching this window, refer to Task 1).

2 Click the **Defragment Now** button in the **Tools** tab.

3 Disk Defragmenter's progress is indicated by the progress bar in the **Defragmenting** dialog box. You can stop or pause the process at any time by clicking the appropriate button.

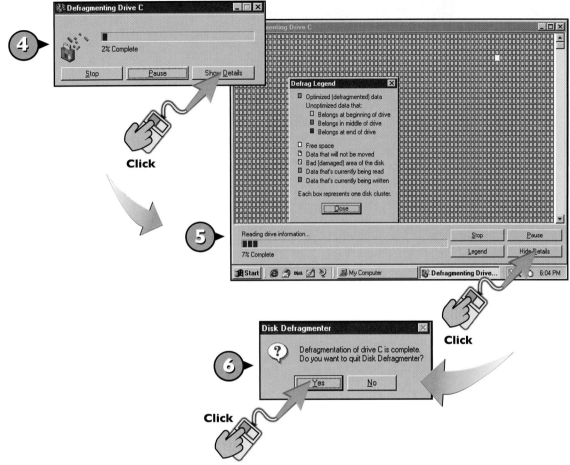

Click

Click

Click

4 ▶ To display details of the process's progress, click the **Show Details** button.

5 ▶ When you are finished viewing the details about the process's progress, click the **Hide Details** button.

6 ▶ When the disk is completely defragmented, click **Yes** to quit. Alternatively, click **No** to return to the **Select Drive** dialog box and defragment another disk.

✅ If the disk does not need to be defragmented, Windows displays a message stating that. You can exit, or you can choose to defragment anyway.

✅ You can access Disk Defragmenter from the Start menu. Click **Start,** choose **Programs,** select **Accessories, click System Tools,** and then choose **Disk Defragmenter.**

End Task

Task 4: Backing Up All Files on Your Computer

Start Here

To safeguard your data, you should back up the files on your system. That way, if something happens to the original, you can restore with this backup or an extra copy. The first time you do a backup, you might want to back up all the files on your system. After you have a complete backup, you can then back up only selected files. Windows includes a backup program you can use. This task covers how to back up all files. The next one covers how to back up selected files.

✓ You can also start the backup program from the **Tools** tab in the **Disk Properties** dialog box.

✓ If backup is critical to your system, you might want to purchase a tape backup system. This method is faster and more convenient than backing up to floppy disks or to a disk file.

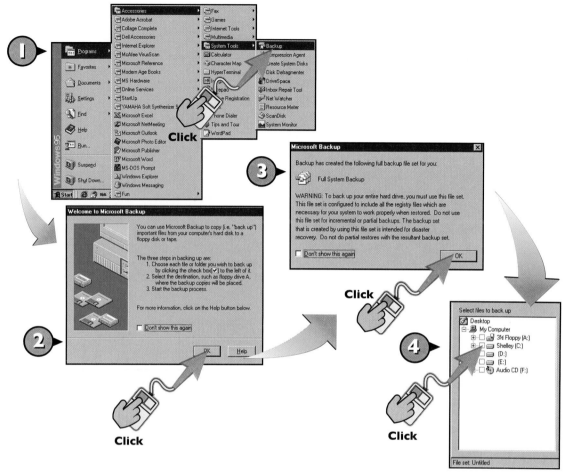

1 Click **Start**, choose the **Programs** command, select the **Accessories** folder, click the **System Tools** folder, and choose **Backup**.

2 In the **Welcome to Microsoft Backup** dialog box, click the **OK** button to go to the first step.

3 Click the **OK** button to confirm that you want to perform a full system backup.

4 Place a check mark next to the drive that contains the files you want to back up.

Next Step

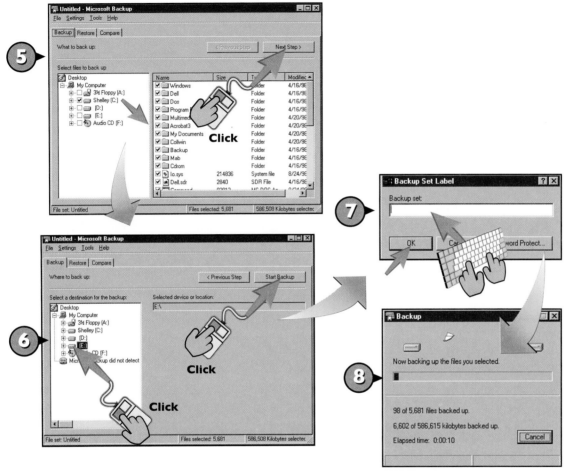

The first time you run backup, you are prompted to set up any backup devices you have. Follow the onscreen instructions.

If you don't want to see the **Welcome to Microsoft Backup** dialog box each time you start the program, check the **Don't show this again** check box in that dialog box.

You can click the **Previous Step** button to go back to the previous step and make a change.

The **Backup Progress** dialog box displays the time elapsed, the files processed, the compression statistics, and other information.

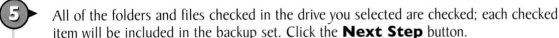

5 ▶ All of the folders and files checked in the drive you selected are checked; each checked item will be included in the backup set. Click the **Next Step** button.

6 ▶ Select where you want to store the backup set, and then click the **Start Backup** button.

7 ▶ Type a name for the backup set (to help you keep track of different backups you make of your system) and then click **OK**.

8 ▶ Watch the backup's progress in the **Backup** dialog box. After you get a message indicating that the backup is complete, click **OK**.

End Task

Task 5: Backing Up Selected Files

You should set up a backup routine that suits you. You might want to back up daily, weekly, or monthly, depending on how often your data is changed and how difficult it would be to recover that data if it was lost. Once you've performed a complete backup, you can then back up selected files (all files that have changed, all files in a particular folder, all files of a certain type, and so on). This task explains how to select which files are backed up.

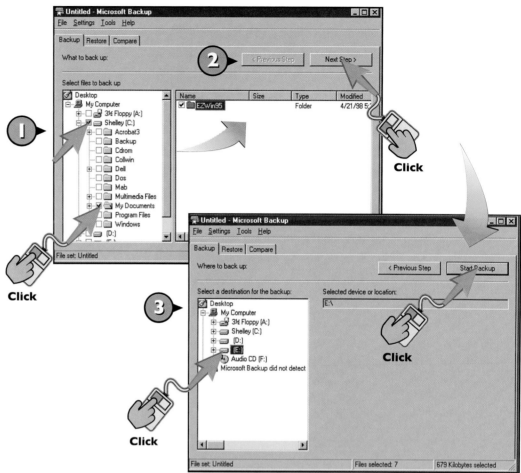

✓ You can expand the folder listing to see any subfolders by clicking the plus sign next to the drive or folder.

1 ▶ Start **Microsoft Backup**. If you need help doing this, refer to the preceding task. Check the folder(s) you want to back up.

2 ▶ Click the **Next Step** button.

3 ▶ Select where you want to store the backup set, and then click the **Start Backup** button.

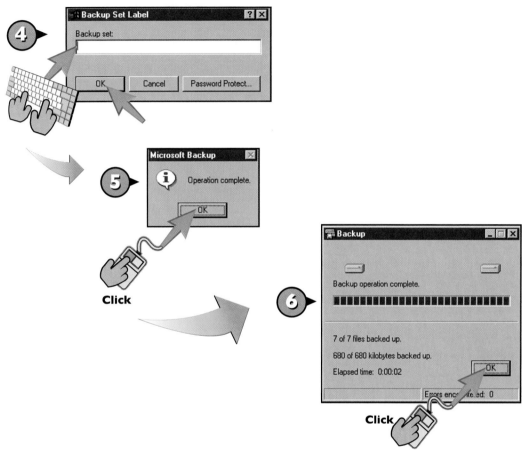

④ Type a name for the backup set (to help you keep track of different backups you make of your system) and then click **OK**.

⑤ When you get a message indicating that the backup is complete, click **OK**.

⑥ Click **OK** to close the **Backup** dialog box.

✅ You can click the **Previous Step** button to go back and make a change to your selections. Click the **Close** button to stop the backup.

✅ The **Backup** dialog box displays the time elapsed, the files processed, and other information.

Task 6: Restoring a Backup

Backup files are stored in a special format. You can't simply copy these files from the backup disks to your hard disk; you must use a special restore procedure. You can restore any files from any of your backup sets.

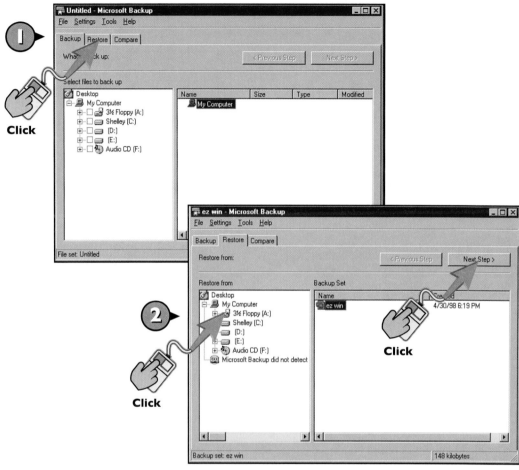

Before you start a restore, make sure you have the disks or tapes with the backup set.

Click the **Restore** tab in the **Microsoft Backup** window (refer to Task 4, "Backing Up All Files on Your Computer," if you need help starting Microsoft Backup).

Select the drive that contains the backup files you want to restore, and then click **Next Step**.

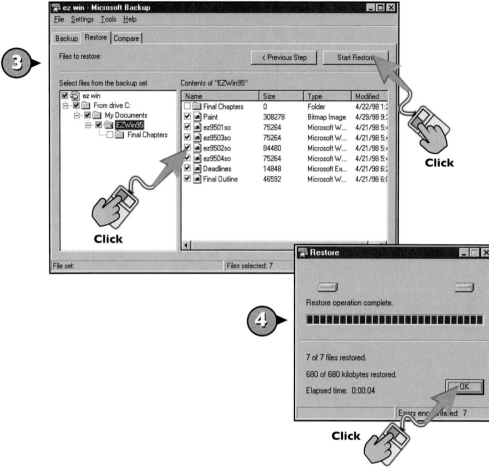

3 Select the files you want to restore from the backup set, and then click the **Start Restore** button.

4 The progress of the restore operation is visible in the **Restore** dialog box. After you are notified that the operation is complete, click **OK** twice, once in each dialog box.

When you restore, you can place the files in the same location or in a different location. You can also select how to handle files that are the same (for example, in the case of a restored version that is identical to a version already on your system).

Task 7: Displaying System Properties

When you are troubleshooting, you sometimes need to display information about your system. You can find this information in the **Properties** dialog box for **My Computer**.

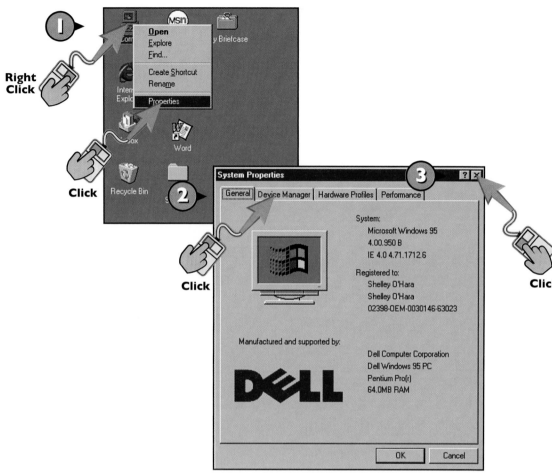

Right Click

Open
Explore
Find...

Create Shortcut
Rename

Properties

Click

Recycle Bin

System Properties

General | Device Manager | Hardware Profiles | Performance |

System:
Microsoft Windows 95
4.00.950 B
IE 4.0 4.71.1712.6

Registered to:
Shelley O'Hara
Shelley O'Hara
02398-OEM-0030146-63023

Manufactured and supported by:

DELL

Dell Computer Corporation
Dell Windows 95 PC
Pentium Pro(r)
64.0MB RAM

OK   Cancel

Click

Click

INFO

1 Right-click the **My Computer** icon and choose **Properties**.

2 Click any of the tabs to display specific system information.

3 When you are finished, click the **Close** button.

Task 8: Formatting a Disk

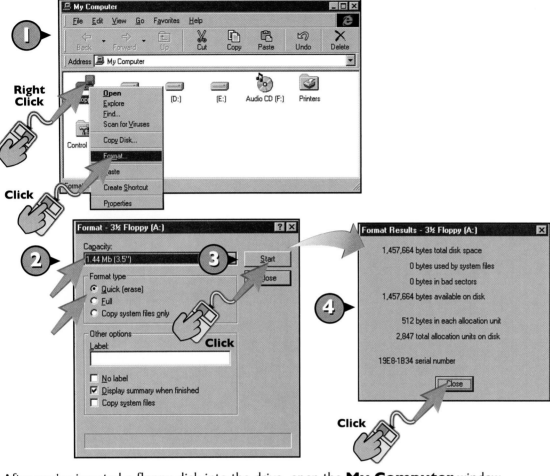

For you to be able to use a floppy disk, that disk must be formatted. Many disks sold are already formatted, but if they are not or if you want to reformat a disk, you can do so. Keep in mind that formatting a disk erases all the information on that disk.

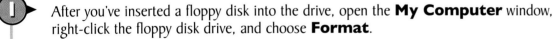

① After you've inserted a floppy disk into the drive, open the **My Computer** window, right-click the floppy disk drive, and choose **Format**.

② Make any changes in the **Capacity** and **Format type** sections (and type a label for the disk if you want).

③ Click **Start**.

④ Windows formats the disk and displays a message with details about the disk. To exit, click the **Close** button twice, once in each dialog box.

✓ You should format a hard disk only in the most extreme circumstances. Remember that formatting a disk erases all information on that disk. If you format your hard disk, everything on it will be wiped out.

✓ For information on creating a startup disk to use to start your system, see the next task.

Task 9: Creating System and Startup Disks

When you start your system, it looks for the appropriate startup files on the floppy drive and then goes to the hard drive. This startup method ensures that if something is wrong with the hard drive, you can always start from a floppy disk. You can make a system disk with the necessary files to keep for emergencies.

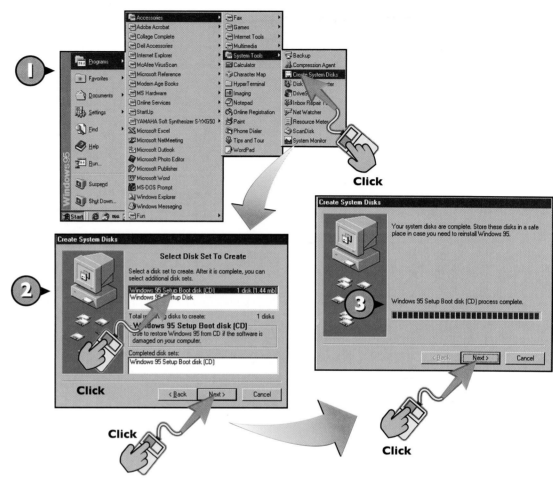

Click

Click

Click

Be sure to use a blank floppy disk or a floppy disk that doesn't contain anything you need. When you create the startup disk, all other information on the disk will be erased.

 Click **Start**, choose the **Programs** command, select the **Accessories** folder, click the **System Tools** folder, and choose **Create System Disks**.

 After you read the overview of the process and click **Next**, select the disk set you want to create. Click **Next** to continue.

 When prompted, insert the disk and click the **Next** button. After the process is complete, click the **Next** button.

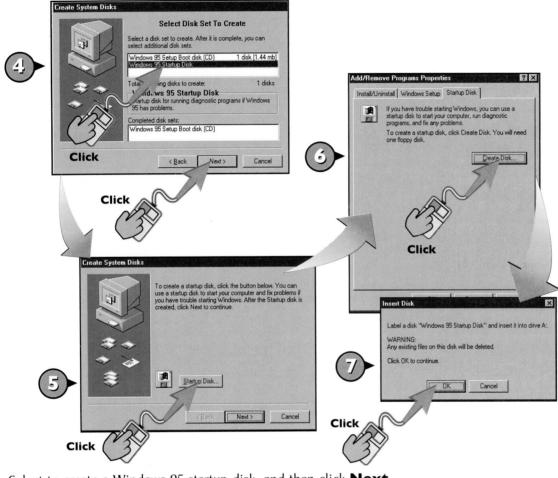

4 ▸ Select to create a Windows 95 startup disk, and then click **Next**.

5 ▸ Click the **Startup Disk** button.

6 ▸ Click the **Create Disk** button.

7 ▸ Insert a blank disk and click **OK**.

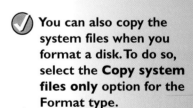 You can also copy the system files when you format a disk. To do so, select the **Copy system files only** option for the Format type.

Task 10: Installing New Hardware

You can install a new printer, modem, or other hardware quickly and easily by using Windows' wizard feature. Windows guides you through questions about the hardware, and if you do not know the answers, Windows can detect the type of hardware and install it with little input from you. Windows calls this handy feature *plug-and-play*. This task shows you how to install hardware.

✓ If the hardware is not automatically detected, you can select to install it manually. Select **No, the device isn't in the list.** Click **Next** and follow the onscreen instructions.

✓ You can choose **Cancel** at any time to stop the process. Click **Back** to go back and change a selection you made.

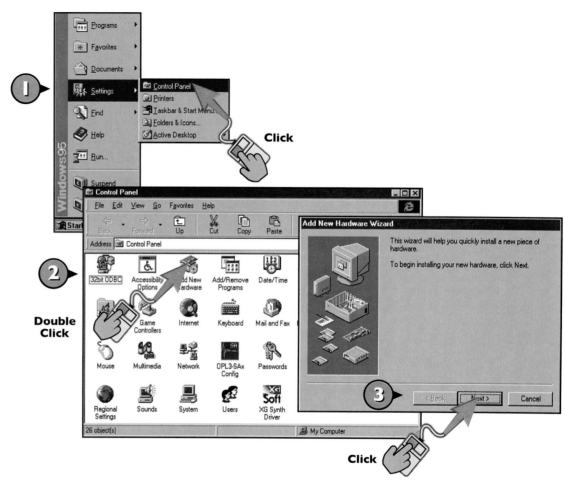

Start Here

Click

Double Click

Click

1 ▶ After you've connected the device to your computer, click **Start**, choose **Settings**, and select **Control Panel**.

2 ▶ Double-click the **Add New Hardware** icon.

3 ▶ Click the **Next** button.

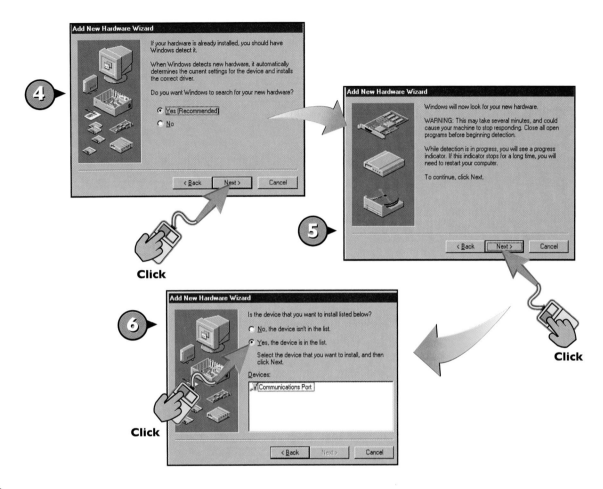

Click

Click

Click

4 When prompted to have Windows search for your new hardware, leave **Yes** selected and click **Next**.

5 Click the **Next** button to continue.

6 Windows searches your system and displays newly installed hardware. Select the device to install from the **Devices** list, and then click **Next**.

✓ Connect the new hardware device to your computer by following the instructions that came with the hardware device.

✓ If Windows detected your hardware, it is set up automatically. You might be prompted to insert the appropriate software disks to set up the hardware. Follow the onscreen directions.

PART 9

Connecting to Online Services and the Internet

If you have a modem and an Internet connection, you can venture beyond your PC to resources available from online services, such as America Online and MSN, or from the Internet. Windows 95 comes with an **Online Services** folder; you can use the icons in this folder to try out any of these services. You might also have Internet Explorer 4, a Web browser that offers you complete and convenient browsing of the Internet. As with any browser software, you can use Internet Explorer 4 to view World Wide Web pages, to search for specific topics, and to download and upload files. In addition to browsing the Web, you can use Internet Explorer 4's mail program, Outlook Express, to exchange email messages with others who are connected to the Internet. You can also use Outlook Express to participate in newsgroups. Finally, if you have a fax modem, you can send and receive faxes.

Tasks

Task 1: Connecting to America Online

America Online (AOL) is the most popular online service company. (It recently purchased another popular online service, CompuServe.) AOL provides content, bulletin boards, email, and other services for subscribers. You can also access the Internet through AOL. Windows 95 conveniently enables you to try out America Online; you can find the **AOL** icon in the **Online Services** folder on your desktop.

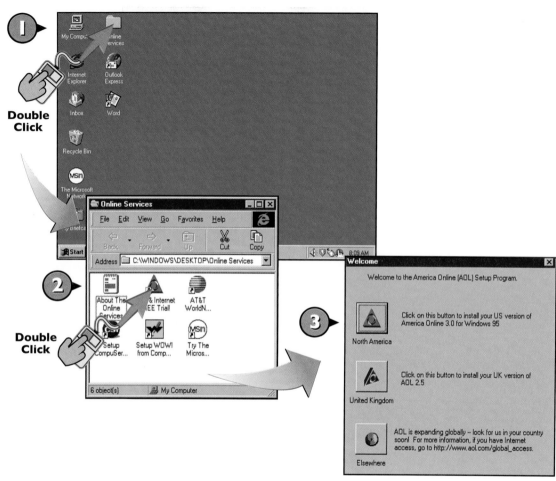

Double Click

Double Click

 Most online providers offer a trial subscription. After that subscription expires, you must pay for the service. Be sure you understand all the fees involved before you sign up.

 You can cancel the setup at any time by clicking the **Cancel** button.

1 ▸ Double-click the **Online Services** icon on the desktop.

2 ▸ To set up America Online, double-click the **AOL** icon.

3 ▸ Follow the onscreen instructions for getting set up.

End Task

Task 2: Connecting to MSN

Start Here

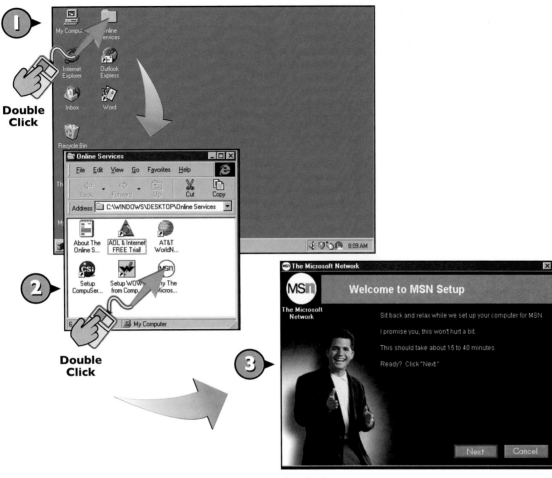

Double Click

Double Click

Another popular online service provider is **Microsoft Network (MSN),** which is managed by **Microsoft. Like America Online, MSN** enables you to view content, participate in forums and other types of discussions such as live chats, send email, and access the Internet. You can find information about this online service provider in the **Online Services** folder.

1 ▶ Double-click the **Online Services** icon on the desktop.

2 ▶ Double-click the **MSN** icon.

3 ▶ Follow the onscreen instructions for getting set up.

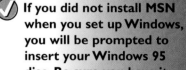 If you did not install MSN when you set up Windows, you will be prompted to insert your Windows 95 disc. Be sure you have it handy.

End Task

Task 3: Setting Up for the Internet

To explore the Internet, you must have a modem and an Internet connection. You can get this connection through online providers such as America Online or MSN, or you can get an account from an independent Internet service provider (ISP). Before you can take advantage of all the benefits of the Internet, you must get your Internet connection set up. Windows makes it easy to set up your Internet connection by providing a wizard that guides you through the steps.

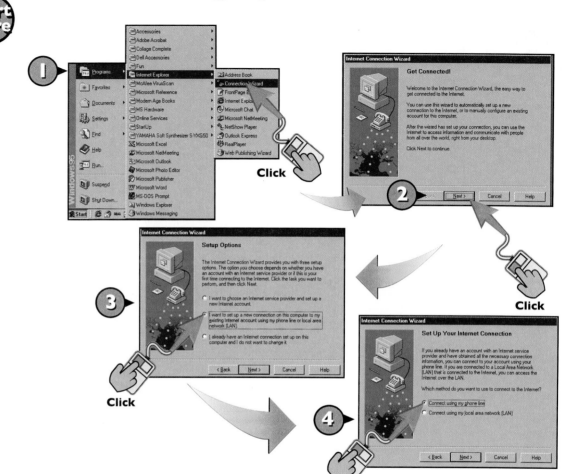

✓ This task assumes that you already have an Internet account.

1 ▸ Click **Start**, choose **Programs**, select **Internet Explorer**, and click **Connection Wizard**.

2 ▸ Click the **Next** button.

3 ▸ If you have an Internet account, click the middle radio button.

4 ▸ Specify how you want to get connected—through your phone line or through your LAN—and then click **Next**.

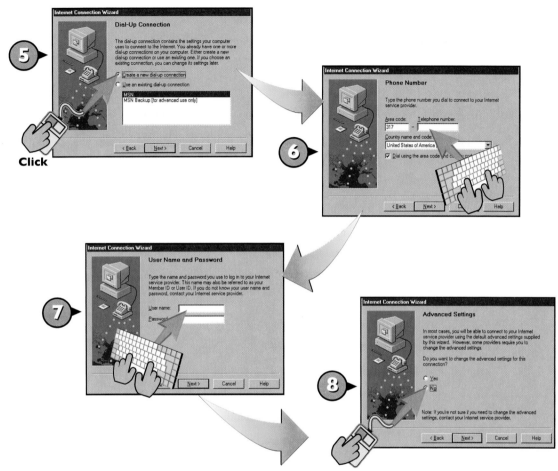

Click

✓ If you do not have an ISP and you want Windows to find one for you, choose **I want to choose an Internet service provider and set up a new Internet account**, and then follow the wizard's directions.

✓ You can find local ISPs in the Yellow Pages. There are also nationwide providers, such as **AT&T WorldNet** (you can get information about this provider from the **Online Services** folder), MindSpring, and EarthLink. Be sure to compare pricing and services when selecting an ISP.

5 ▶ Select to use an existing dial-up connection or to create a new one (this task assumes you want to create a new one), and then click **Next**.

6 ▶ Type the telephone number you use to connect to your Internet service provider and click **Next**.

7 ▶ Type your user name and the password assigned to you by your ISP, and then click **Next**.

8 ▶ If you do not want to change the advanced settings (this task assumes you don't), click **No**, and then click **Next**.

Next Step

Page
211

Setting Up for the Internet Continued

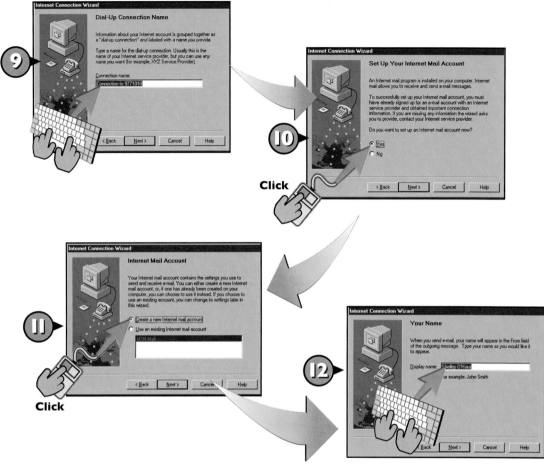

Click

Click

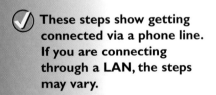
These steps show getting connected via a phone line. If you are connecting through a LAN, the steps may vary.

Type a name for your dial-up connection (you can use any name you want), and then click **Next**.

Select **Yes** if you want to set up your Internet mail account (this task assumes that you do), and then click **Next**.

Specify whether you want to use an existing account or create a new account (this task assumes you want to create a new one), and then click **Next**.

Type the name you want displayed in outgoing messages, and then click **Next**.

Next Step

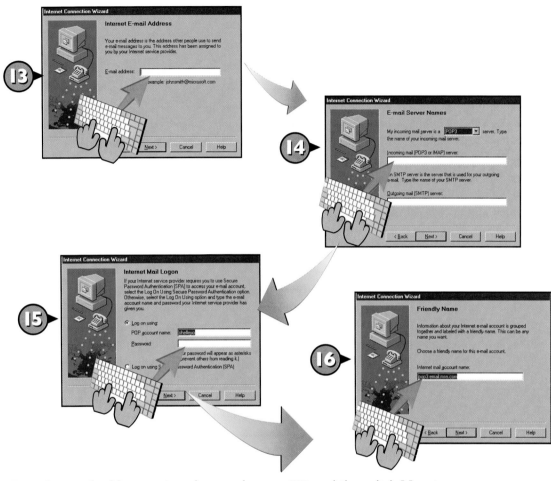

13 Type the email address assigned to you by your ISP, and then click **Next**.

14 Enter the requested information about your incoming and outgoing mail servers (you can get this information from your ISP), and then click **Next**.

15 Specify logon instructions, and then click **Next**.

16 Type a name for the mail account, and then click **Next**.

✓ **If you need to change one of your selections, click the Back button to go back through your choices.**

✓ **To cancel the setup, click the Cancel button.**

Setting Up for the Internet Continued

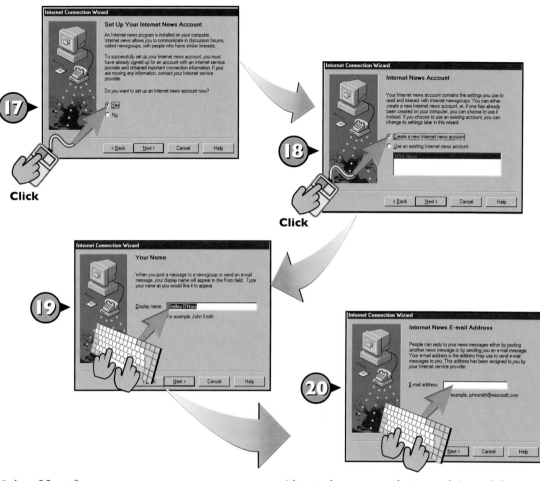

Click

Click

17 ▶ Select **Yes** if you want to set up a news account (this task assumes that you do), and then click **Next**.

18 ▶ Specify whether you want to use an existing account or create a new account (this task assumes you want to create a new account), and then click **Next**.

19 ▶ Type the name you want displayed in messages posted to the newsgroup, and then click **Next**.

20 ▶ Type the email address assigned to you by your ISP, and then click **Next**.

Next Step ▶

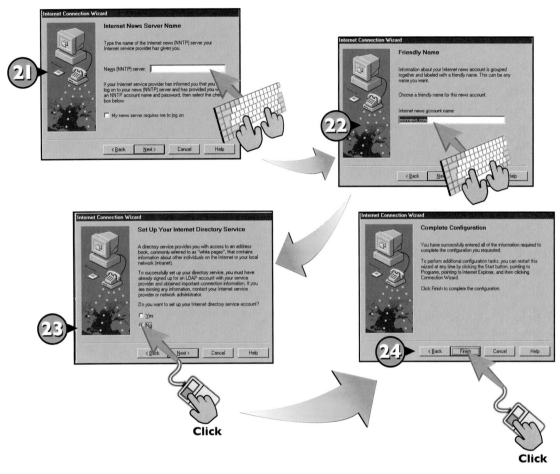

Click

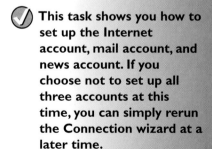

Click

21 Enter the requested information about your news server (you can get this information from your ISP), and then click **Next**.

22 Type a name for the news account, and then click **Next**.

23 Select **No** when prompted to set up an Internet directory service account, and then click **Next**.

24 Click the **Finish** button to complete the setup.

 This task shows you how to set up the Internet account, mail account, and news account. If you choose not to set up all three accounts at this time, you can simply rerun the Connection wizard at a later time.

End Task

Task 4: Starting Internet Explorer

Once you've got your Internet connection set up, you can start Internet Explorer and browse the Internet.

Start Here

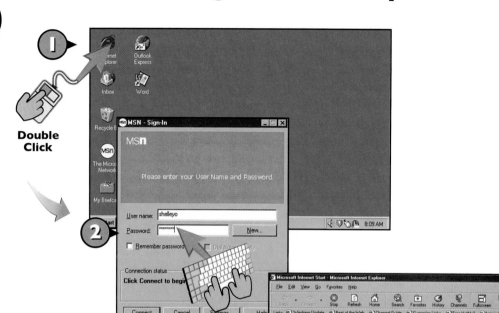

Double Click

Click

 You return to the start page (also called the home page) at any time by clicking the **Home** button.

 If you have problems connecting—the line is busy, for instance—try again. If you continue to have problems, check with your ISP.

1 Double-click the **Internet Explorer** icon.

2 Enter your user name and password (some information might have been completed for you), and then click the **Connect** button.

3 Windows connects to your ISP. The **Internet Explorer** window appears, and you see your start page, usually the Microsoft home page.

 End Task

Task 5: Browsing with Links

Start Here

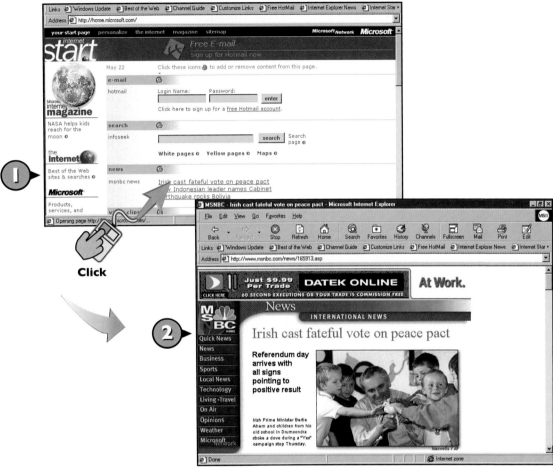

Click

Information on the Internet is easy to browse because documents contain *links* to other pages, documents, and sites. Simply click a link to view the associated page. You can jump from link to link, exploring all types of topics and levels of information. Links are also called *hyperlinks*, and usually appear underlined and sometimes in a different color.

If you see an error message when you click a link, it could indicate that the link is not accurate or that the server is too busy. Try again later.

Images can serve as links. You can tell whether an image (or text) is a link by placing your mouse pointer on it; if the pointer changes into a pointing hand, the image (or text) is a link.

Because the Microsoft home page is updated frequently, the links you see will be different from the ones shown here.

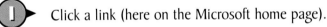
Click a link (here on the Microsoft home page).

The page for that link appears (in this case, a news story on **www.msnbc.com**).

End Task

Task 6: Typing an Address

Typing a site's address is the fastest way to get to that site. An address, sometimes called a *URL* (uniform resource locator), looks like this: **http://www.nba.com**. The first part is the protocol (usually **http://** for Web pages). Next you have the domain name (**www.nba**) and then the extension (usually **.com, .net, .gov, .edu**, or **.mil**), which indicates the type of site (commercial, network resources, government, educational, or military, respectively).

 If you get an error message, make sure you typed the address correctly. You must type the periods, colons, slashes, and other characters in the exact order.

 New with Internet Explorer 4 is a feature called *AutoComplete*. If you have typed an address before, you can type only its first few letters; Internet Explorer will display the rest.

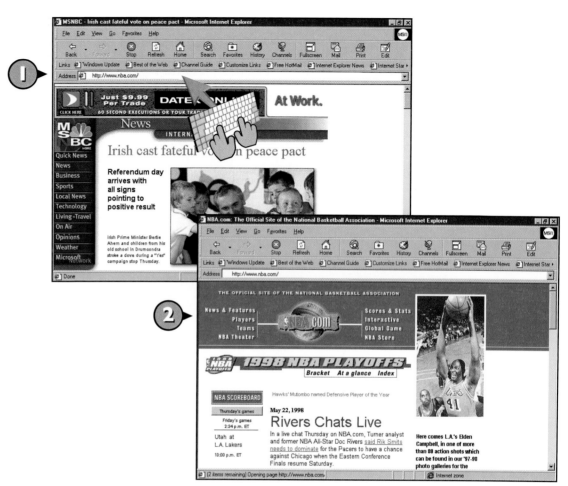

In the **Address** bar, type the address of the site you want to visit (I've typed **www.nba.com**), and then press **Enter**.

Internet Explorer displays the page associated with the URL you typed (in this case, the page for the NBA).

Task 7: Browsing with Toolbar Buttons

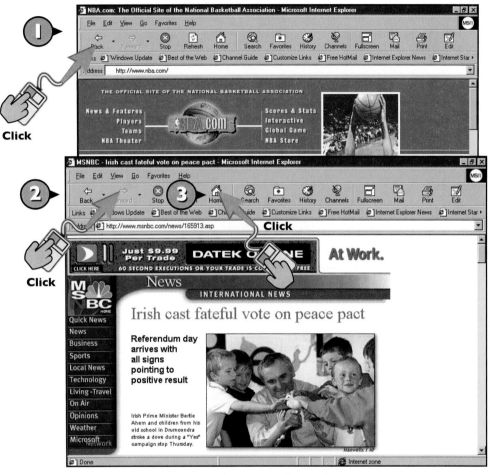

Click

Click

Click

When you click on a link or type an address, you journey from page to page. To help you navigate among the pages, you can also use the buttons on the toolbar. You can go back to pages you have previously viewed, forward through pages after going back, and back to your start page.

✅ Click any of the buttons in the **Links** toolbar to see some sites selected by Microsoft. You can select to view sites in several categories.

✅ You must have clicked the **Back** button before you can use the **Forward** button.

1 ▶ From the NBA page, click the **Back** button in the toolbar.

2 ▶ You go back to the last page you viewed (here the Microsoft home page). Click the **Forward** button to move forward through the pages you've already visited.

3 ▶ To return to the Microsoft start page after moving forward through pages you've visited, click the **Home** button in the toolbar.

Task 8: Adding a Site to Your Favorites List

When you find a site that you especially like, you might want a quick way to return to it without having to browse from link to link or having to remember the address. Fortunately, Internet Explorer 4 enables you to build a list of favorite sites and to access those sites by clicking them in the list.

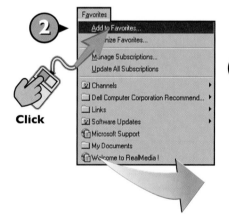

Click

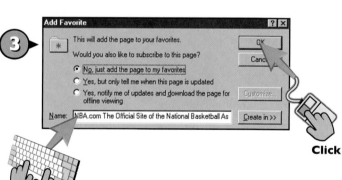

Click

✓ You can subscribe to sites and be alerted when the content has been updated. See the online help for information about subscribing to a site.

✓ You can set up Internet Explorer to download the site so that you can review the information offline. Less time online can mean smaller ISP bills!

 Open the Web site that you want to add to your **Favorites** list.

 Click the **Favorites** option in the menu bar (do not click the **Favorites** button in the toolbar), and choose the **Add To Favorites** command.

 Type a name for the page if you're not satisfied with the default name that is provided, and then click **OK**. The page is added to your list.

End Task

Task 9: Going to a Site in Your Favorites List

After you have added a site to your **Favorites** list, you can easily reach that site by displaying the list and selecting the site.

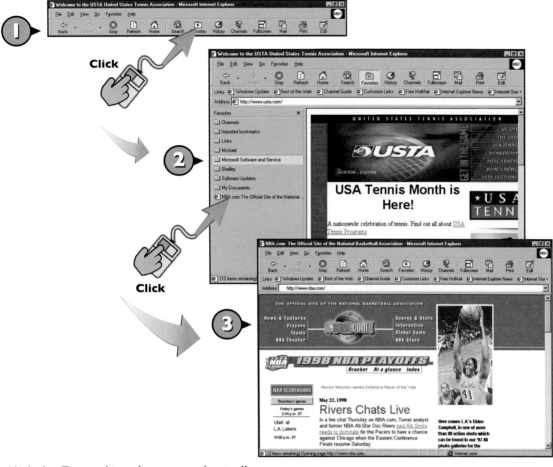

Click

Click

To close the **Favorites** pane, click its **Close** button.

1. Click the **Favorites** button on the toolbar.

2. The pane on the left side of the screen contains your **Favorites** list, while the right-hand pane contains the current page. Click the site you want to visit.

3. Internet Explorer displays the site you selected from the **Favorites** list (in this instance, the NBA page).

You can also reach a site by opening the **Favorites** menu and selecting the folder and site you want. For more information on adding folders, see the next task.

End Task

Task 10: Rearranging Your Favorites List

If you add several sites to your **Favorites** list, it might become difficult to use. You can organize the list by grouping similar sites together in a folder. You can add new folders and move sites from one folder to another.

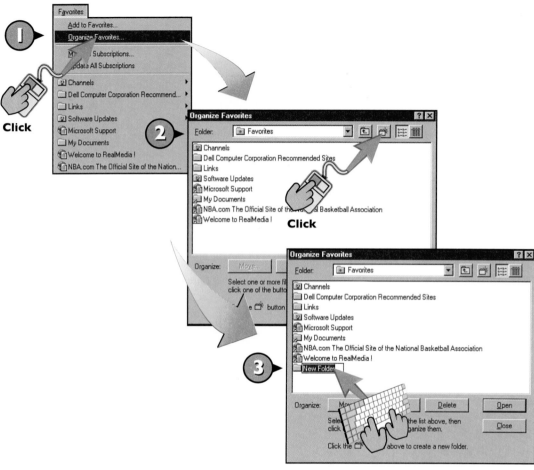

Start Here

Click

Click

Organize Favorites

Folder: Favorites

- Channels
- Dell Computer Corporation Recommended Sites
- Links
- Software Updates
- Microsoft Support
- My Documents
- NBA.com The Official Site of the National Basketball Association
- Welcome to RealMedia !

Organize: Move...

Select one or more fil
click one of the butto

Organize Favorites

Folder: Favorites

- Channels
- Dell Computer Corporation Recommended Sites
- Links
- Software Updates
- Microsoft Support
- My Documents
- NBA.com The Official Site of the National Basketball Association
- Welcome to RealMedia !
- New Folder

Organize: Move...   Delete   Open

Sele...   the list above, then   Close
click...   ganize them.

Click the   above to create a new folder.

✓ You can drag a site from the list to the folder where you want to place the site.

1 ► Click the **Favorites** option in the menu bar and then choose **Organize Favorites**.

2 ► To create a new folder, click the **New Folder** button.

3 ► The new folder is created. Type the folder name and press **Enter**.

Next Step

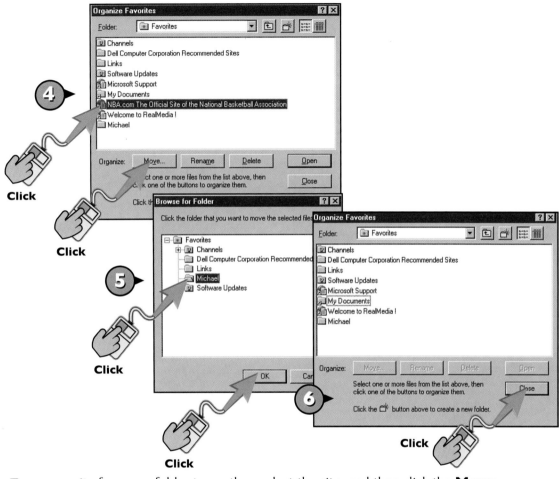

Click

Click

Click

Click

Click

Click

4️⃣ To move a site from one folder to another, select the site, and then click the **Move** button.

5️⃣ Select the folder into which you want to move the site, and then click **OK**.

6️⃣ When you are finished moving all the sites you want to rearrange, click the **Close** button.

✅ To delete a site, select it and click the **Delete** button. Click the **Yes** button to confirm the deletion.

✅ To rename a site, select the site and click the **Rename** button. Type a new name, and press **Enter**.

Task 11: Reviewing Web Channels

A new way of receiving content is to have it delivered to you via a *channel*. You can select to view a channel at any time. You also can subscribe to a channel and have the content downloaded at the interval you specify. Several companies are creating content specifically for Internet Explorer; expect this list to grow as more and more content providers get involved.

Click

Click

Click

✓ You can also access these channels from your desktop. To display the channels, click the **View Channels** button in the **Quick Launch** toolbar.

✓ To close the channel bar, click its **Close** button.

1 ▶ Click the **Channels** button in the toolbar.

2 ▶ Click **Microsoft Channel Guide**.

3 ▶ The Microsoft Active Channel Guide is displayed in the right-hand pane of the **Internet Explorer** window.

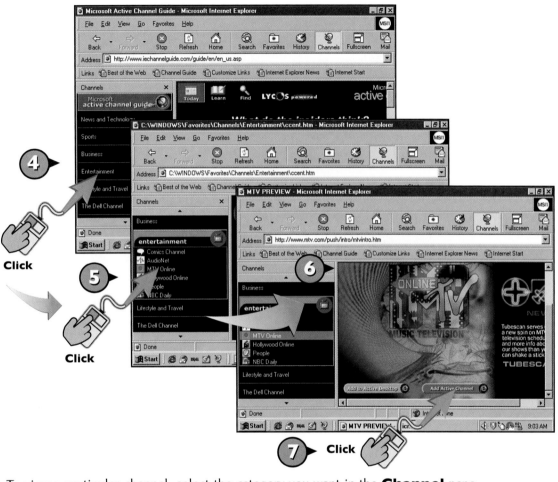

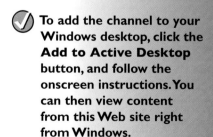

4 To view a particular channel, select the category you want in the **Channel** pane.

5 Click the channel you want to view.

6 You see a preview of the channel in the right pane.

7 To add this channel to your Active Channel Guide, click the **Add Active Channel** button, and then follow the onscreen instructions.

Click

Click

 Click

To add the channel to your Windows desktop, click the **Add to Active Desktop** button, and follow the onscreen instructions. You can then view content from this Web site right from Windows.

End Task

Task 12: Searching the Internet

The Internet includes many, many, *many* different sites. Looking for the site you want by browsing can be like looking for a needle in a haystack. Instead, you can search for a topic, and find all sites related to that topic. To search, you select to use either a search engine or a search index. The basic procedure is the same, but the results and special options for each search engine/index will vary.

✓ You can refine a search and set search options. You can also find more information about the site, such as reviews or ratings, from some search tools. The search tool usually lists the "best" matches first. Look for a link at the end of the list to display the next set of matches.

✓ If you don't find the topic you want, you can try a different search engine. The results may be different.

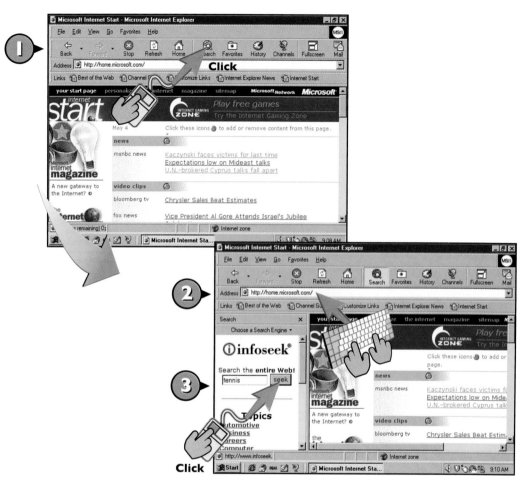

 Click the **Search** button in the toolbar.

 In the **Search** bar that appears along the left-hand side of the screen, type the word or phrase you want to find.

 Click the **seek** button. (The name of the button will vary depending on which provider you use.)

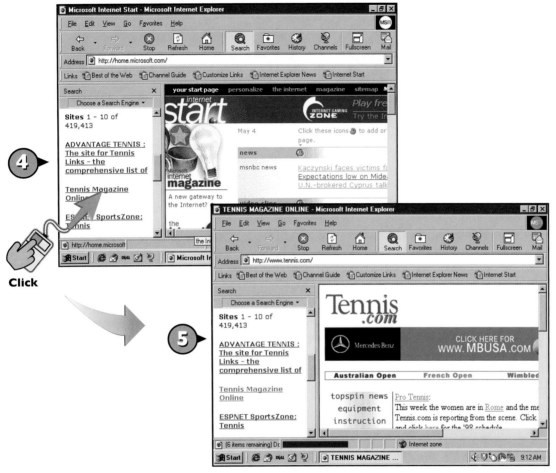

 4 The left pane displays the results of the search in link format. Scroll down until you find the link you want, and then click it.

 5 The page you selected appears in the right-hand pane.

Click

You can scroll through the search bar pane to see all the results. To close the search bar, click its **Close** button.

To select a different search engine, click the **Choose a Search Engine** drop-down list and click the tool you want to use. You can display a list of all search engines by selecting this item from the list. Then select the tool you want from the pane on the right.

Task 13: Setting Internet Security Levels

With Internet Explorer 4, you can assign different zones to various sites, and assign a security level to each zone. Assign the **Local** zone to sites on your intranet; assign the **Trusted** zone to any sites from which it is safe to download and run files; assign the **Restricted** zone to sites from which it is not safe to download and run files. The **Internet** zone is assigned to all other sites by default. A site's assigned zone is displayed in the status bar.

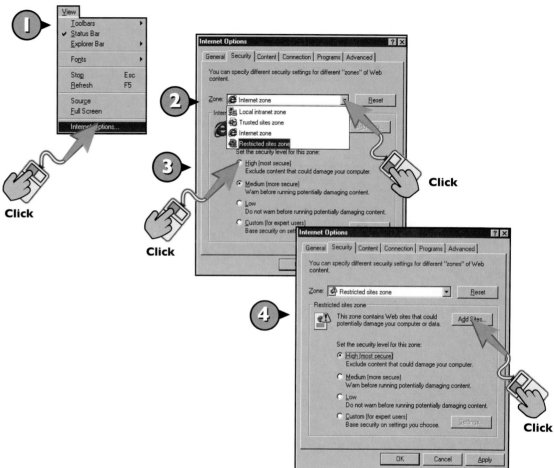

(✓) For more information on security, review the online help. Internet Explorer 4 devotes an entire section of its help system to security issues.

1 To view information about zones or to alter the settings of a zone, click **View**, and then choose **Internet Options**.

2 To set the security level for a zone, select it in the **Zone** drop-down list box in the **Security** tab of the **Internet Options** dialog box.

3 Click either the **High**, **Medium**, **Low**, or **Custom** radio button in the **Internet zone** section.

4 To add Web sites to a particular zone, select the zone in the **Zone** drop-down list and click the **Add Sites** button.

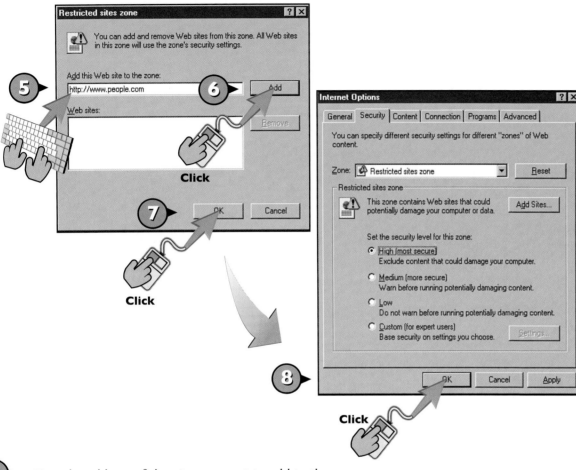

Click

✓ To remove a site from a zone, choose **View**, and then select **Internet Options**. Click the **Security** tab, display the zone assigned to the site you want to remove, and then click the **Add Sites** button. Select the site to be removed and click the **Remove** button. Click **OK** twice to exit the dialog boxes.

✓ Repeat steps 5 and 6 for each site you want to add to the zone.

5 ▶ Type the address of the site you want to add to the zone.

6 ▶ Click the **Add** button.

7 ▶ Click **OK** to return to the **Internet Options** dialog.

8 ▶ After you finish assigning security levels, click the **OK** button in the **Internet Options** dialog box.

End Task

Task 14: Using the History List

As you browse from link to link, you might remember a site that you liked, but not remember that site's name or address. You can easily return to sites you have visited by displaying the **History** list. From this list, you can select the week you want to review, and then the site you want to visit.

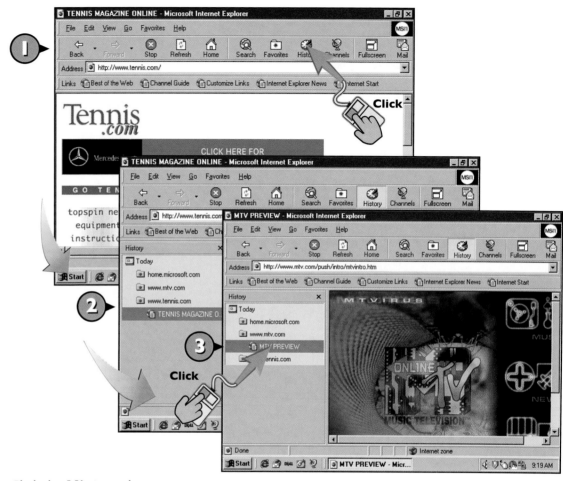

Click the **History** button.

To close the **History** list, click the **Close** button in the top-right corner of the **History** pane.

You can select how many days the history is kept, and you can clear the **History** list. Choose **View**, click **Internet Options**, and then select the number of days the history should be kept. To clear the history, click the **Clear History** button.

Click the **History** button.

Internet Explorer displays the **History** list in a pane on the left side of the window. If necessary, select the week whose list you want to review.

Click the site you want (you might have to click a few folders to reach the site). Internet Explorer displays that site.

Task 15: Exiting Internet Explorer

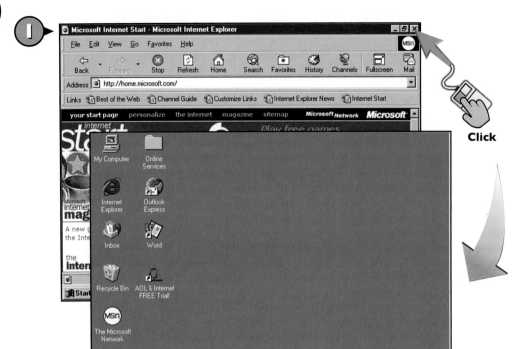

Click

Click

When you are finished browsing the Internet, you need to exit Internet Explorer and also close your connection to your Internet provider.

 To exit, click the **Close** button in the upper-right corner of the **Internet Explorer** window.

 Right-click the Internet connection icon in the status bar and choose **Disconnect** to close your ISP connection.

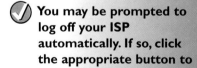 You may be prompted to log off your ISP automatically. If so, click the appropriate button to end the connection.

Task 16: Starting Outlook Express

Start Here

You can use Outlook Express to create, send, receive, and reply to email over the Internet. You can also send files—such as reports, spreadsheets, pictures, and so on—by attaching them to your messages.

✓ To use Outlook, your computer must be configured for use over the Internet. Refer to Task 3, "Setting Up for the Internet," if you need help doing this.

✓ The first time you run Outlook Express, you will be prompted to select the dial-up connection and mail folders. Simply make your selections in the dialog boxes that appear.

✓ Depending on how Outlook Express is set up on your computer, you might also be connected to your Internet provider, and your mail might be automatically checked— that is, you don't have to select a command to check the mail.

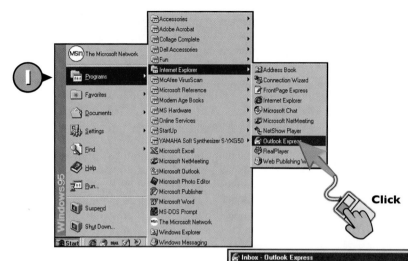

I

Click

2

I ▶ Click **Start,** choose the **Programs** command, select **Internet Explorer**, and then click **Outlook Express**.

2 ▶ Outlook Express is started.

End Task

Task 17: Reading Mail

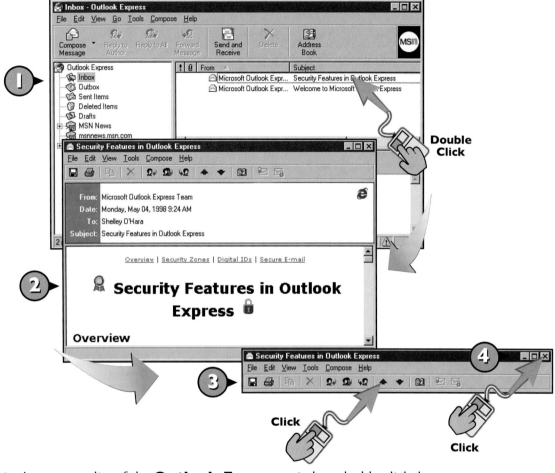

Double Click

When you start Outlook Express and get connected to your Internet provider, all incoming messages are downloaded from your Internet mail server to your computer's inbox. The message list (the upper-right pane) lists all messages. Messages appearing in bold have not yet been read, but you can open and read any message in the message list (whether it is bold or not).

Click

Click

✓ To print an open message, choose **File**, select **Print**, and then click **OK** in the **Print** dialog box. To save an open message, choose **File** and then click **Save As**. In the **Save As** dialog box, assign the message a filename and location, and then click **Save**.

1 ▶ In the message list of the **Outlook Express** window, double-click the message you want to read.

2 ▶ The message you selected is displayed in its own window. You can scroll through the contents to read the message.

3 ▶ To display the next message in the message list, click the up-arrow button in the toolbar. To display the previous message in the message list, click the down arrow.

4 ▶ To close the message, click the **Close** button.

✓ To delete a message, select the message. Then choose **File** and click **Delete**, or click the **Delete** button in the toolbar.

Task 18: Creating and Sending Mail

Start
Here

You can send a message to anyone with an Internet email address. Simply type the recipient's email address, a subject, and the message. You can also send carbon copies (Cc) and blind carbon copies (Bcc) of messages, as well as attach files to your messages.

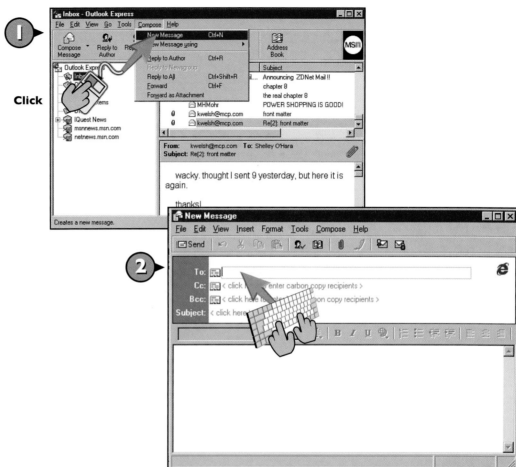

Click

✓ You can also click the **Compose Message** button in the toolbar to create a new message.

✓ If you enter an incorrect address and the message is not sent, you most likely will receive a **Failure to Deliver** notice. Be sure to type the address in its proper format.

1 In the **Outlook Express** window, click **Compose** and then choose **New Message**.

2 Type the recipient's address (as well as any necessary Cc and Bcc addresses). Addresses are in the format **username@domainname.ext** (for example, **sohara@msn.com**). Press **Tab**.

Next Step

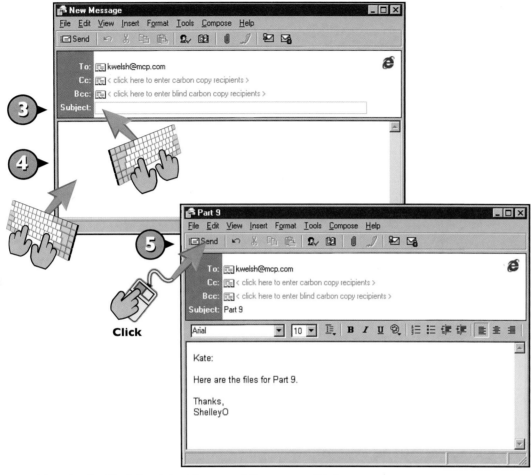

Click

Type a subject in the **Subject** text box, and then press **Tab**.

Type your message.

When you've completed the message, click the **Send** button.

✓ Providing a subject in Outlook Express is mandatory.

✓ To attach a file—such as a spreadsheet or word-processing document—to your message, choose **Insert** and then click **File Attachment**, or click the **Insert File** button. In the **Insert Attachment** dialog box, choose the file you want to attach and click the **Attach** button.

✓ If you are connected to the Internet, the message is sent when the **Send** button is clicked. If you're not connected to the Internet, Windows places the message in the **Outbox**, where it remains until the next time you connect to your ISP. You can connect and send the message by clicking the **Send and Receive** button.

Task 19: Responding to Mail

You can easily respond to a message you've received. Outlook Express completes the address and subject lines for you; you can then simply type the response.

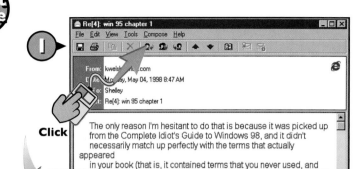

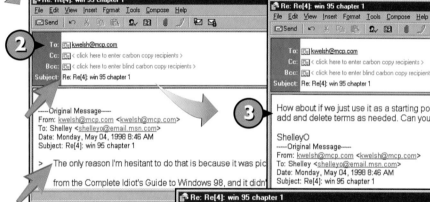

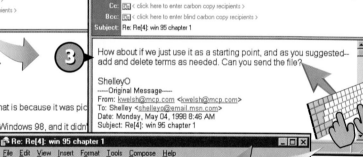

Click

✓ You can also click the **Reply to Author** command in the **Compose** menu.

✓ To forward a message, click the **Forward** command in the **Compose** menu, or click the **Forward** button on the toolbar. Type the address of the recipient, click in the message area, and type any message you want to include. Click the **Send** button.

Click

1 ▶ Display the message to which you want to reply, and click the **Reply to Author** button in the toolbar.

2 ▶ The address and subject lines are completed, and the text of the original message is appended to the bottom of the reply message.

3 ▶ Type your message.

4 ▶ Click the **Send** button.

End Task

Task 20: Subscribing to Newsgroups

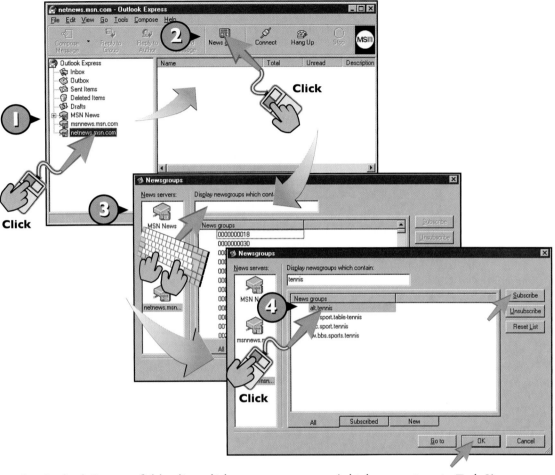

A *newsgroup* is a collection of messages relating to a particular topic. Anyone who subscribes to the newsgroup can view and respond to posted messages and also post new messages. You can join any of hundreds of thousands of newsgroups on the Internet. You use Outlook Express for both email and newsgroups.

✓ The first time you select to view your newsgroup, you are prompted to view a list of the available newsgroups. Follow the onscreen instructions for viewing and subscribing to a newsgroup.

✓ You can search for a specific word—for example, **computers** or **banjo**—by entering the word in the **Display Newsgroups Which Contain** text box.

✓ To unsubscribe to a newsgroup, click the **News groups** button. Select the newsgroup to which you want to unsubscribe and then click the **Unsubscribe** button.

① In the Outlook Express folder list, click your news server (which you set up in Task 3).

② Click the **News groups** button in order to subscribe to a newsgroup.

③ To narrow the list of newsgroups, type the name of a topic area that interests you in the **Display newsgroups which contain** text box.

④ Select a newsgroup from the **News groups** list, click the **Subscribe** button, and click **OK**.

Task 21: Reading Newsgroup Messages

After you have subscribed to a newsgroup, you can review any of the messages in that group. When a new message is posted, it starts a *thread*, and all responses are part of this thread. You can review all the current messages in the thread.

Start Here

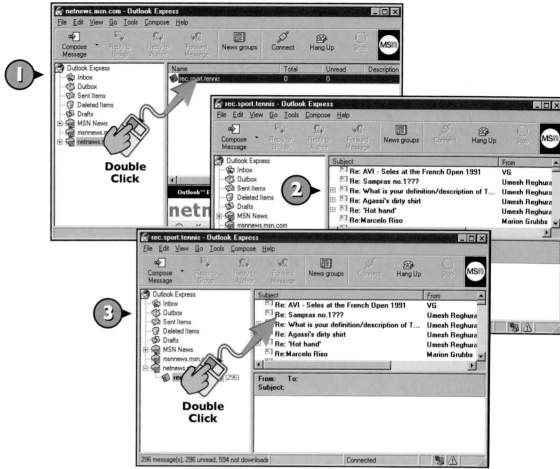

Double Click

✓ **Keep in mind that newsgroups are not usually monitored. You might come across messages that you find offensive. If so, it's best to just unsubscribe from that newsgroup.**

1 ▶ Double-click the newsgroup you want to review.

2 ▶ A list of that newsgroup's messages appears in the message list. Messages in bold have not yet been read; messages with a plus sign have responses.

3 ▶ Double-click the message you want to read (in this case, **Sampras no. 1???**).

Next Step

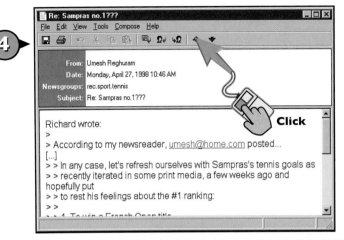

4 The message is displayed in its own window. To display the next message, click the up-arrow button in the toolbar; to display the previous message, click the down-arrow button.

5 To close the message, click the **Close** button.

 To print a message, select it in the window, click File and choose Print. To save a message, select it, click File, and then choose Save Message. Then assign the message a location on your hard drive and click OK.

Task 22: Posting New Messages

After you review messages, you might want to post your own. One way to do this is to post a new message (that is, start a new thread).

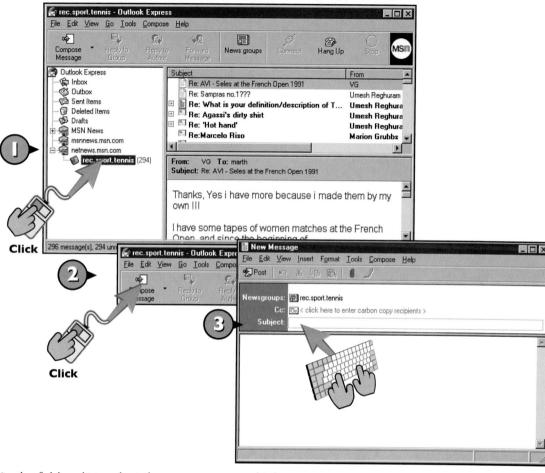

In the folders list, select the newsgroup to which you want to post a new message.

Click the **Compose Message** button.

Type a subject in the subject line of the **New Message** dialog.

Next
Step

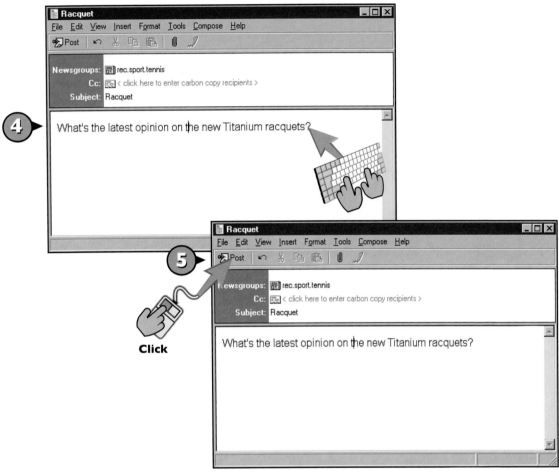

Click

Type your message.

Click the **Post** button on the toolbar.

If you change your mind about posting a message, you can cancel the message if you have not already clicked Post. Simply click the message's **Close** button and, when prompted, click the Yes button to confirm that you don't want to save the message.

Task 23: Replying to an Existing Newsgroup Message

Start Here

If you come across a newsgroup message to which you want to respond, you can post a reply to that message.

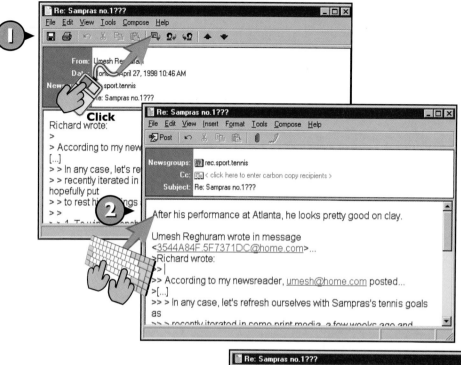

Click

Click

✓ You can also reply to messages privately by emailing the author. To send an email message, click the **Reply to Author** button. Type your message, and click the **Send** button.

① ▶ Display the message to which you want to reply, and click the **Reply to Group** button.

② ▶ Type your message.

③ ▶ Click the **Post** button.

End Task

Task 24: Closing Outlook Express

Start Here

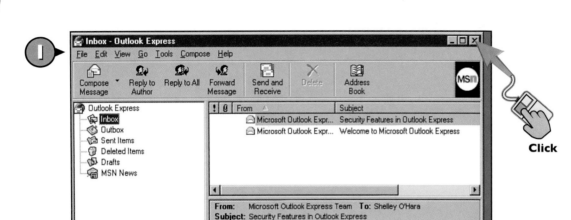

Click

When you are finished reading and sending mail, you need to exit Outlook Express and also close your connection to your Internet provider.

To exit, click the **Close** button in the upper-right corner of the **Outlook Express** window.

 Click Yes if you are prompted to log off your ISP connection.

End Task

Task 25: Setting Up Microsoft Fax

If you have a fax modem, you can send and receive faxes using Microsoft Fax, a program included with Windows 95. You can use this program to compose, send, and receive faxes. To use this program, you must first set up some information about your phone line and fax modem. You set up this information in a Microsoft Exchange profile. Microsoft Exchange is a program that can handle faxes as well as email.

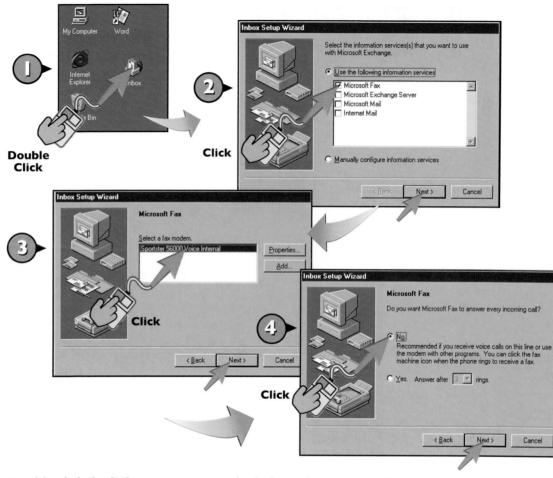

✓ You don't have to use Microsoft Fax to compose, send, and receive faxes. If you have another fax program that came with the modem or that you purchased separately, you can use it to fax.

1 ▶ Double-click the **Inbox** icon to start the **Inbox Setup** wizard.

2 ▶ Check only **Microsoft Fax**, and click **Next**.

3 ▶ Select the fax modem and click **Next**.

4 ▶ Select how to handle incoming calls and click **Next**.

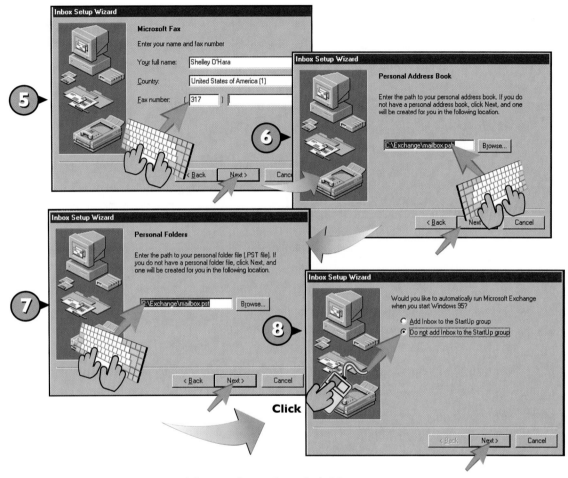

5 Enter your name, country, and fax number. Then click **Next**.

6 Enter the path to your address book or simply click **Next** to create a new one.

7 Enter the path to your personal folder file or simply click **Next** to create a new one.

8 Select whether you want to add Microsoft Exchange to your **StartUp** folder and click **Next**. Click the **Finish** button in the next dialog to complete the setup.

✓ You can also start the **Inbox Setup** wizard by starting any program that requires it, such as **Microsoft Fax.**

✓ You can use the Microsoft **Exchange Server** to handle email, but you most likely will use Outlook Express, which is included with Internet Explorer 4, as your mail program. For more information on using Microsoft Exchange, consult online help.

Task 26: Composing and Sending a Fax

Once you've set up the fax, you can send a fax to anyone who has a fax line. You create the document using your PC and then fax it to another fax machine or another PC with a fax modem. Windows 95 includes a fax wizard that leads you step by step through the process of creating a fax.

✓ If you have a fax modem, you cannot fax hard-copy versions of documents. You can only fax documents you have created electronically.

✓ If you have set up your fax modem to fax from more than one location, you will be prompted to select the location after step 3. Click the location and then click **Next.** You can turn off this message by checking the **I'm not using a portable computer, so don't show this to me again** check box.

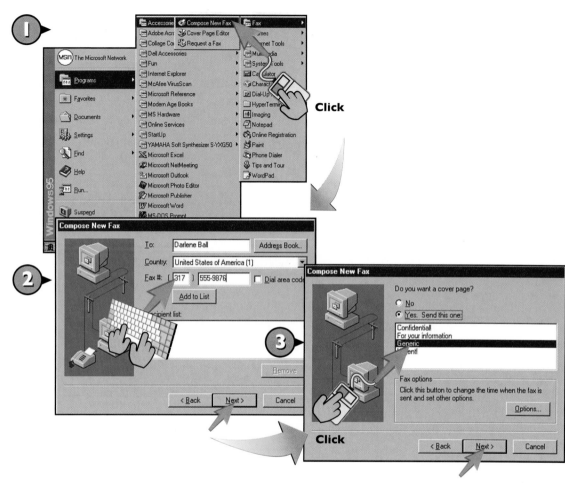

1 ▶ Click **Start**, choose **Programs**, select **Accessories**, click **Fax**, and then choose **Compose New Fax**.

2 ▶ Type the name of the recipient and the fax number. Click **Next**.

3 ▶ Select the cover page you want to use and click **Next**.

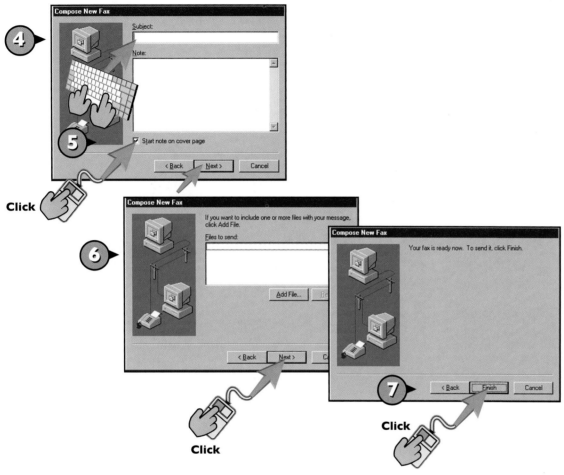

Click

Click

Click

④ ► Type the subject and note.

⑤ ► To start the note on the cover page, check **Start note on cover page**. Click **Next**.

⑥ ► Click **Next** to skip adding a file.

⑦ ► Click **Finish** to send the fax.

✓ You can set up an address book of fax numbers and then select the recipient from the list. To view the address book, click the **Address Book** button.

✓ You can attach a file to send along with the fax. To do so, click the **Add File** button and then select the file.

End Task

Task 27: Receiving and Viewing a Fax

You can also use Microsoft Fax to receive faxes from others. You can view them onscreen and also print them. To receive a fax, Microsoft Exchange, a program used to handle faxes and email, must be running. You can set up Microsoft Fax to answer automatically, or you can answer manually (as covered here).

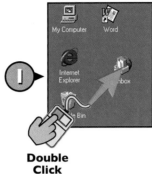

Start Here

Double Click

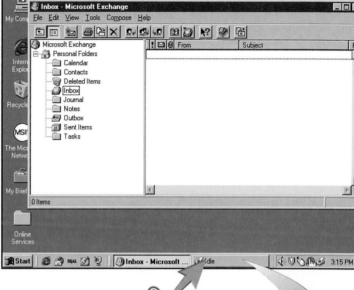

Double Click

Click

✓ Use the buttons in the Microsoft Exchange toolbar to print, delete, and save faxes.

✓ To set Microsoft Fax to answer automatically, click **Tools**, choose **Microsoft Fax Tools**, and then select **Options**. Click on the **Modem** tab. On this tab, click the **Properties** button and then select how to answer in the **Answer mode** section. Click **OK** twice.

 Double-click the Microsoft Exchange **Inbox** icon.

 Double-click the **Fax** icon in the taskbar.

 Click the **Answer Now** button.

Next Step

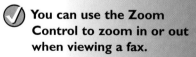

You can use the Zoom
Control to zoom in or out
when viewing a fax.

4 Microsoft Fax displays the status of the incoming fax and then places it in Microsoft
Exchange's inbox. Double-click the fax to view its contents.

5 You see the fax onscreen. Click the **Close** button to exit Microsoft Fax.

A

accessory One of the mini-applications that comes free with Windows 95. Examples include WordPad, Paint, and Backup. Accessories can be found in the **Accessories** menu.

active window The window you're currently using. You can tell a window is active by looking at its title bar. If the bar shows white letters on a dark background, the window is active. Inactive windows show light gray letters on a dark gray background.

address Also called the *URL* or *uniform resource locator*. An address is the designation of a Web site. A Web address usually consists of the protocol, domain name, and extension. Here is an example: **http://www.nba.com**.

application Software that accomplishes a specific practical task such as creating documents. It's the same thing as a *program*.

application window A window that contains a running application, such as Explorer or WordPad.

B

backup The process of saving an extra copy of the files on your system so that you can restore them if anything happens to the original. Windows 95 includes Microsoft Backup, a program you can use to create backups.

boot To start your computer.

browser A program that you use to view sites on the World Wide Web. The browser that comes with Windows 95 is called Internet Explorer.

C

CD-ROM drive A special computer disk drive that's designed to handle CD-ROM disks, which resemble audio CDs. CD-ROMs have enormous capacity (about 500 times that of a typical *floppy disk*).

channel A special World Wide Web site that features changing content that is sent automatically to your computer at predefined intervals.

check box A square-shaped switch that toggles a dialog box option on or off. The option is toggled on when a check mark appears in the box.

classic view   The folder view used with Windows 95. That is, you click an icon to select it, and you double-click an icon to launch it. See also *Web view*.

click   To quickly press and release the left mouse button.

Clipboard   An area of memory that holds data temporarily during cut-and-paste operations.

cluster   A physical division of the hard drive. When saving a file, Windows finds the first available cluster and places in it as much of the file that will fit. Then Windows goes to the next cluster, and so on, until the entire file is written to the disk.

command button   A rectangular "button" on the screen that, when clicked, runs whatever command is spelled out on it.

commands   The options you see in a pull-down menu. You use these commands to tell the application what you want it to do next.

D

desktop   A metaphor for the Windows 95 screen.

device driver   A small program that controls the way a device (such as a mouse) works with your system.

dialog boxes   Windows that pop up on the screen to ask you for additional information about how to perform a command and to seek confirmation of an action you requested.

directory   See *folder*.

diskette   See *floppy disk*.

document window   A window opened in an application. Document windows hold whatever you're working on in the application.

double-click   To quickly press and release the left mouse button *twice* in succession.

double-click speed   The maximum amount of time Windows 95 allows between the mouse clicks of a double-click.

drag   To press and hold down the left mouse button and then move the mouse.

drag-and-drop   A technique you use to run commands or move things around; you use your mouse to *drag* files or icons to strategic screen areas and *drop* them there.

drop-down list box   A list box that normally shows only a single item but, when selected, displays a list of options.

E

email   Short for *electronic mail*. A typed message sent through the phone lines to someone else with an email account. You can use Outlook Express, which is the email program included with Internet Explorer, to send email messages.

F

fax modem   A special type of modem that enables you to fax documents created on your PC to other fax modems or machines. You can also receive faxes and print them on your printer.

file   An organized unit of information inside your computer.

floppy disk   A portable storage medium that consists of a flexible disk protected by a plastic case. Floppy disks are available in a variety of sizes and capacities.

folder   A storage location on your hard disk in which you keep related files together.

font   A character set of a specific typeface, type style, and type size.

format   The process of setting up a disk so that a drive can read its information and write information to it.

format bar   A series of text boxes and buttons that enable you to format the characters in your WordPad document. The format bar typically appears under the toolbar.

fragmented   When a single file is divided and stored in separate chunks scattered around a hard disk. You can fix this by running Windows 95's Disk Defragmenter program.

H

hard disk   The main storage area inside your computer.

hyperlink   See *link*.

I

icons   The little pictures that Windows 95 uses to represent programs and files.

insertion point   The blinking vertical bar you see inside a text box or in a word-processing application, such as WordPad. It indicates where the next character you type will appear.

Internet A *network* of networks that extends around the world. By setting up an account with an Internet service provider, you can access this network.

Internet Explorer A browser created by Microsoft that you can use to view information on the Internet. The latest version is Internet Explorer 4.

Internet service provider (ISP) A company that provides access to the Internet. You connect to this provider via your phone line and pay the company for your connection time.

intranet The implementation of *Internet* technologies for use within a corporate organization rather than for connection to the Internet as a whole.

ISP See *Internet service provider*.

K

keyboard An input device used to type text, enter values, select commands, and otherwise communicate with the PC.

keyboard shortcut A key combination that you can press to select a command. If you prefer to keep your hands on the keyboard, you can use keyboard shortcuts rather then the mouse to open a menu and select a command. For example, you can use the following keyboard shortcuts for moving around in WordPad:

Press	**To move...**
←	One character left
→	One character right
↑	Up one line
↓	Down one line
Home	To the start of the line
End	To the end of the line
Ctrl+Home	To the top of the document
Ctrl+End	To the end of the document

L

LAN See *local area network*.

local area network A *network* in which all the computers occupy a relatively small geographical area, such as a department, office, home, or building. All the connections between computers are made via network cables.

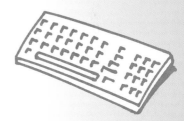

link   A special text entry or image on a Web page that represents another page. You can click the link to go to the new page. Links usually appear in a different color and underlined on a Web page. Also called *hyperlinks*.

list box   A small window that displays a list of items such as filenames or folders.

M

maximize   To increase the size of a window to fill the entire window.

menu bar   The horizontal bar in an application window that contains the application's pull-down menus.

minimize   To remove a program from the desktop without closing it. A button for the program remains on the taskbar.

modem   An electronic device that enables two computers to exchange data over phone lines.

N

network   A collection of computers connected via special cables or other network media to share files, folders, disks, peripherals, and applications. See also *local area network*.

newsgroup   An Internet discussion group devoted to a single topic. These discussions progress by members "posting" messages to the group.

O

option buttons   See *radio buttons*.

P

plug and play   A Windows technology that enables you to easily add hardware to your system. For plug and play components, Windows automatically recognizes the new hardware and then configures your system so that you can use the new hardware.

pop-up menu   See *shortcut menu*.

point   To place the mouse pointer so that it rests on a specific screen location.

port　The connection into which you plug the cable from a device such as a mouse or printer.

print queue　A list of print jobs that have been sent to the printer and are waiting to be printed.

program　See *application*.

pull-down menus　The list of menu commands that you can display by clicking on the menu name in the menu bar.

R

radio buttons　Dialog box options that appear as small circles in groups of two or more. Only one option from a group can be chosen. These are also called *option buttons*.

RAM　Stands for random-access memory. The memory in your computer that Windows 95 uses to run your programs.

resolution　The measure of the crispness of an image. Can apply to a printed image and to what you see on your monitor.

restore　The process of copying backup files to your system so that you can use the files.

right-click　To click the right mouse button instead of the usual left button. In Windows 95, right-clicking something usually pops up a *shortcut menu*.

S

screen saver　A moving graphic that is displayed on your monitor if the computer is inactive for a certain amount of time (you specify how long). Windows 95 includes a few screen savers that you can use.

scrollbar　A bar that appears at the bottom or on the right side of a window when the window is too small to display all its contents. You can use the scrollbar to view the other contents of the window.

shortcut　A special file that points to a program or a document. Double-clicking the shortcut starts the program or loads the document.

shortcut menu　A menu that contains a few commands related to an item (such as the *desktop* or the *taskbar*). You display the shortcut menu by *right-clicking* the object.

spin box　A special type of numerical text box. You can type an entry or use the spin arrows to increase or decrease the increment.

subscribe   The process of joining a newsgroup so that you can review messages and post your own.

subscription   A method of checking for new or changed data on a World Wide Web site or *channel*. The subscription sets up a schedule for checking a particular site to see whether it has changed in any way since the last time it was checked.

T

tab   A page of options in a dialog box.

taskbar   The horizontal strip across the bottom of the Windows 95 screen. Each running application is given its own taskbar button, and you switch to an application by clicking on its button.

text box   A screen area in which you type text information, such as a description or a filename.

text editor   A program that lets you edit files that contain only text. The Windows 95 text editor is called Notepad.

title bar   The area on the top line of a window that displays the window's title.

toolbar   A series of application-specific buttons that typically appears beneath the menu bar.

U

uniform resource locator (URL)   See *address*.

URL   See *address*.

W

Web   Short for World Wide Web. The Web is the graphical presentation of information on the Internet. You can browse from page to page by clicking on *links*.

Web view   The folder view you use to browse your desktop and system contents like a Web page. For instance, you single-click an icon to launch it. See also *classic view*. You can use Web view if you have Internet Explorer 4.

wildcard   A character used to represent any single character or any group of characters. For instance, in the filename **CH*.DOC**, the ***** character acts as a wildcard to indicate all files that start with **CH** and have a **.DOC** extension.

window   A rectangular screen area in which Windows 95 displays applications and documents.

wizard   A Windows feature that leads you step-by-step through a particular process. For instance, you can use the Add Printer wizard to set up a new printer.

word wrap   A word-processor feature that automatically starts a new line when your typing reaches the end of the current line.

C

copying

D

Edit menu commands

G - H

I - J - K

Index

W